# The
# Gold Rush

Based on the Public Television Series

# THE WEST

# The Gold Rush

## by Liza Ketchum

*With an Introduction by Stephen Ives and Ken Burns*

Little, Brown and Company

BOSTON    NEW YORK    TORONTO    LONDON

*For John, who shared every step of the journey with me*

•◆• •◆• •◆•

## Acknowledgments

Thanks to the staffs of the American Antiquarian Society in Worcester, Massachusetts, the Huntington Library in San Marino, California, and Primary Source in Cambridge, Massachusetts, for invaluable assistance with research. I am also grateful to the following friends, family members, and colleagues for help with the manuscript and in tracking down primary source material: Eileen Christelow, Janet Coleman, Dayton Duncan, Karen Hesse, Dick Ketchum, Deborah Kovacs, Katherine Leiner, Joy and Todd Lewis, Bob MacLean, Derek and Ethan Murrow, Rosie Shiras, John Straus, Vicki Gohl, and Avi Wortis. Special thanks to Jackie Horne, Gail Hochman, and Carl Brandt for their encouragement and good counsel throughout the project.

First Edition

Photography credits appear on page 118.

Library of Congress Cataloging-in-Publication Data

Ketchum, Liza.
     The gold rush / Liza Ketchum ; based on the Public Television series
*The West*; with an introduction by Stephen Ives and Ken Burns. — 1st ed.
          p.     cm.
     Summary: Illustrates the event that drew thousands of people to
California and its effect on the gold seekers, the Spanish settlers,
and the native Indian tribes who lived there.
     ISBN 0-316-59133-5 (hc)
     ISBN 0-316-49047-4 (pb)
     1. California — Gold discoveries — Juvenile literature. 2. Gold
mines and mining — California — History — 19th century — Juvenile
literature. [1. California — Gold discoveries. 2. Gold mines and
mining — California — History — 19th century.] I. Title.
F865.K4 1996
979.4'01 — dc20                                                        95-43210

10 9 8 7 6 5 4 3 2

Q-KP

Published simultaneously in Canada by Little, Brown & Company (Canada) Limited
and in Great Britain by Little, Brown and Company (UK) Limited

Printed in the United States of America

# Contents

# Introduction

**M**omentous events that change the world often begin with ordinary people doing ordinary things. The small group of workers who were building a sawmill on California's American River during the winter of 1848 had no idea that their picks and shovels would loosen a glittering gold nugget from the gravel. And they never imagined how one tiny golden chunk could unleash a frenzied desire for wealth that would speed around the globe, luring a quarter of a million people with the cry of "Gold! Gold in California!"

Like the television series on which it is based, *The Gold Rush* tells the story of the individual men, women, and children who traveled to California to seek their fortunes—and of the Native Americans and Spanish-speaking Californios whose lives were turned upside down when thousands of miners appeared from every corner of the world.

Many gold seekers knew they were taking part in a historic migration. They described their experiences in diaries and letters, made sketches showing life in the mines, or used one of the earliest photographic techniques, called the daguerreotype, to capture the faces of people who were making history. These precious records, guarded carefully by their descendants and now residing in libraries and museums, provide us with intimate details of what life was like in covered wagons and on clipper ships. They allow us to experience firsthand the exhausting labor of digging for gold, the bustle of life in San Francisco, the painful homesickness of living among strangers. *The Gold Rush* draws heavily on this rich and personal source material.

Just as important to this period in our history are the stories of the people who left few records behind: Chinese immigrants whose letters

home remain in China; Native Americans who didn't live long enough to pass their stories on to their children; Californios whose pleas for justice were ignored by those who seized their *ranchos*.

Although a few people who made the journey to California became wealthy or famous, most of the men, women, and children who experienced the gold rush disappeared into the shadows of history. But we hope you will share our feeling that their ordinary lives became extraordinary because they helped shape an era that would change the West—and the United States—forever.

—Stephen Ives and Ken Burns

# A World Turned Upside Down

*James Marshall at
Sutter's mill*

It was wash day at the site of a new sawmill in Coloma, California. Jennie Wimmer, the cook and laundress for the construction crew, was making soap in her big lye kettle. The workmen had finished their excavations for the day, and Jennie's four children were playing in the channel the men had dug in the swift-moving American River. Suddenly Jennie heard a commotion outside. Her son, John, rushed up, followed by James Marshall, the foreman at the construction site. They showed Jennie a small, bright stone, found in the channel of the millrace. Could it be gold?

Eagerly they compared the nugget to a gold coin, but the colors didn't match. How could they test it?

Jennie knew what to do. As she later recalled: "I said, ... 'I will throw it into my lye kettle ... and if it is gold, it will be gold when it comes out.'"

Jennie dropped the nugget into the cloudy water, then finished her soap and put it aside to cool. The next morning, she reached into the bottom of her pot, "and there was my gold, as bright as could be."

## *Gold! Gold! Gold from the American River!*

*— Sam Brannan, May 12, 1848*

James Marshall took credit for the discovery. But did he really pluck the nugget from the millrace, as he claimed? Did Nisenan Indians working under Marshall find the first chunks of gold? Or was it young John Wimmer, whose family always claimed that he had dug the first shining nugget from the gravel of the riverbed?

No matter who made the discovery, the small stone was really gold. A tiny nugget no bigger than a dime, discovered on January 24, 1848, would change the West forever.

*John Sutter*

John Sutter, a wealthy German-born settler, claimed ownership of the Nisenan land where the sawmill was being constructed. When he heard about the gold, Sutter rode forty-five miles from his fort to the mill site, where Peter Wimmer, Jennie's husband, presented him with four ounces of gold collected by their children. Other workers showed Sutter flecks and nuggets they had found as they deepened the channel that would turn the mill wheel. Some bit into the gold to test it, while others hammered the chunks to make sure they didn't flake, as fool's gold did.

Sutter was worried. His fort was the center of trade for all the settlers in the Sacramento River valley, where he owned more than fifty thousand acres of land. He had visions of ruling an empire he called Nueva Helvetia, or New Switzerland, in honor of the country where he had lived as a young man. The discovery of gold could ruin his plans, so he begged his mill workers to keep it a secret.

But Sutter himself couldn't help boasting to his friend, the wealthy ranchero Mariano Guadalupe Vallejo, about the riches that lay hidden on his land. And as construction of the mill loosened more gold from the sand and gravel, the news spread slowly, like a fire smoldering undetected. In California in 1848, there was no telephone or telegraph, no television or radio. There were no trains between the East and West Coasts and no overland mail routes. Letters and newspapers took weeks, or even months, to reach their destination.

Nine days after the find at Sutter's mill, Mexico ceded California to the United States as part of a treaty ending the Mexican-American War. The treaty was signed near Mexico City; no one meeting there knew that the rivers and streams of northern and central California would soon yield a fortune in gold. In fact, neither country thought much of California. To Americans, California was a dangerous, semiarid wilderness, inhabited by hundreds of native tribes. American pioneers were more likely to choose the Oregon Territory for its fertile land than California.

And as far as Mexico was concerned, its former province was a back-water, suitable for thieves and scoundrels. When the United States and Mexico had been at war, the Mexicans had hardly bothered to send troops to defend California. Mexico didn't think much about how the new treaty might affect the few thousand Californios, Mexicans who had settled in the province. Most raised cattle in California's grassy valleys, sending the hides to shoe factories in Boston.

While Mexico signed away a region rich in gold and minerals, news of the discovery at Sutter's mill traveled by word of mouth. It moved from one isolated *rancho* to the next. It spread into narrow mountain valleys, home to Nisenan, Miwok, Yokut, Pomo, and Maidu Indians, and into small coastal towns, where the smoldering fire suddenly caught, as if fanned by a fierce wind. Gold! There was gold in the streambeds, in the riverbanks, under boulders! Gold, free for the taking!

> *The blacksmith dropped his hammer, the carpenter his plane, the mason his trowel, the farmer his sickle, the baker his loaf, and the tapster his bottle. All were off for the mines.*
>
> — *Reverend Walter Colton, alcalde of Monterey*

Men abandoned stores and businesses. Californios caught *la fiebre del oro*, gold fever, and left their animals untended. Native people waded into the rivers where they usually caught salmon, using shallow baskets to wash the gold from soil and gravel. At Sutter's Fort, where John Sutter employed hundreds of Native Americans, workers began to disappear, and Sutter complained that "even my cook has left me."

By May, half the inhabitants of nearby Monterey had gone to "the diggings," as miners called the mountain regions where they would dig for

*This Minnesota schoolteacher, decked out for the mines, never left home.*

gold. One of the few businesses remaining open was a blacksmith's shop, whose owner couldn't keep up with the demand for picks, shovels, and gold pans. A man writing to friends in the East described the mania for gold as a highly contagious disease. "The whole population are going crazy," he wrote. "Old as well as young are daily falling victim to the gold fever."

Word reached San Francisco, a village of only eight hundred people, but no one believed it until April, when miners swaggered into town, showing off bags full of gold dust. Sam Brannan, a newspaper publisher, went to the mines to see what all the fuss was about. On May 12, he returned to San Francisco and strode through the streets, brandishing a bottle of gold dust and shouting, "Gold! Gold! Gold from the American River!"

Gold fever spread faster than an epidemic. Observers estimated that between two thirds and three quarters of the men in San Francisco disappeared by June. The town's only school, serving about sixty children, closed: The teacher locked the doors and took his pupils to the mines. When only one hotel remained open, its African-American manager demanded—and received—the unusually high salary of seventeen hundred dollars a year. Sailors left whaling vessels stranded in San Francisco's harbor. Soldiers deserted their camps.

*Sam Brannan*

*An extra edition of the NEW YORK HERALD in January 1849 announced the gold discovery.*

In August, California's military governor, Richard B. Mason, and his lieutenant, William Tecumseh Sherman, visited the Mormon Island gold camp on the American River. They filled a tea caddie with gold dust and sent it by sea to President Polk in Washington.

Meanwhile, word spread to the neighboring province of Sonora, in Mexico (where gold had been discovered and mined a few years earlier) and to the thinly populated Oregon Territory. The invasion of California was about to begin.

Ever since the sixteenth century, when Spaniards began to explore the Americas, tall tales about a mythical kingdom of wealth called El Dorado had haunted the West. For this reason, few residents of the eastern United States believed the rumors about gold that trickled into their towns and cities in the fall of 1848. But in December, four months after the tea caddie full of gold dust left San Francisco, it arrived on President Polk's desk in Washington. The president put the gold on display at the War Department and announced to Congress that there was enough gold in California to pay for the war with Mexico.

Newspapers across the country finally picked up the story. By the start of the new year, cities and towns everywhere buzzed with the news. The *New York Herald* began carrying the story on the front page, under the bold headline YELLOW FEVER. Steamships were fitted up for the journey. Thousands of men and some women announced their intention to make the long and dangerous trip to the West Coast. The *Herald*'s front page headline became HO! FOR CALIFORNIA! and its classified section filled with ads for tickets on sailing ships, for mining tools, and for portable houses that could be assembled in California.

**THE WAY THEY GO TO CALIFORNIA.**

*This lithograph made fun of those with "gold fever."*

People imagined instant wealth. As one would-be miner wrote, "A frenzy seized my soul.... Piles of gold rose up before me." B. P. Kloozer, a soldier stationed in California, was torn between duty to his country (which paid him a meager six dollars a month) and the lure of the diggings, where he might make as much as $150 in a day. "I hate to desert," he wrote to his brother in Boston. "I am almost crazy.... Excuse this letter, as I have the 'gold fever' shocking bad."

*I am almost crazy.... Excuse this letter, as I have the "gold fever" shocking bad.*

— B. P. Kloozer

News of the gold discovery gradually spread beyond North America, drawing dreamers and prospectors to California from every corner of the world.

Why did they come? Why did so many people embark on a journey that was as dangerous and incomprehensible as a trip to Mars would be for us

7

*Panning for gold*

today? Many seized on the idea of easy money, sure their problems would be magically solved. Gold seekers left famine in Ireland and fled from economic depression and revolution in Europe. They traveled from Chile and other countries in Latin America; took passage on boats leaving Honolulu, Hawaii; Liverpool, England; Paris, France. Thousands of Chinese left a war-torn country to find the land they called Gum San, or Gold Mountain. In 1848, fewer than fourteen thousand non-Indian people lived in California. Four years after the discovery at Sutter's mill, nearly a quarter of a million people had poured into the new state.

The gold rush turned life upside down. Children who had led sheltered lives in the East helped support their families in California. Women who had never held a job outside the home earned more money feeding the miners than their husbands did panning for gold. African Americans came to California as slaves, earned enough money to buy their freedom, and started their own businesses. Men who had been trained as bankers, lawyers, or doctors spent their days knee-deep in freezing water, moving stones until their hands and feet were numb, while their wives, left behind in the East, found new ways to support their families. Many inventive businessmen and women made fortunes without ever going near the diggings. Others lost money, ruined their health, or died before they even reached the goldfields.

For many thousands of people, the gold rush was an adventure, a chance for a new life. But for those who lived in California before 1849, the gold rush was a catastrophe. In just a few years, many Spanish-speaking Californios lost their land to American miners—land they themselves had seized from Native Americans.

*A soldier will give his captain the slip at the first chance. I don't blame the fellow a whit; seven dollars a month, while others are making two or three hundred a day!*

*— Reverend Walter Colton, alcalde of Monterey*

For the native people of California, the discovery of gold on their land brought an end to their way of life. Many of the first Californians lived in the steep mountain valleys where gold was found. In the invasion that followed, thousands of Native Americans died from diseases spread by the miners. Prospectors kidnapped native children, destroyed their acorn crops, burned native villages, and murdered whole families. Mining killed the fish in the rivers as well as the oak trees growing along their banks. At the beginning of the gold rush, about 150,000 Native Americans lived in California. Twelve years later, less than thirty thousand remained. It was the worst slaughter of native people in American history.

# The First Californians

*An early drawing shows Native Americans welcoming Spanish explorers.*

**I**n 1602, nearly 250 years before the discovery of gold at Sutter's mill, three Spanish galleons sailed into a beautiful bay on the California coast. Their captain, Sebastián Vizcaíno, put ashore on a beach where bears had devoured a whale carcass during the night. There he met a group of people his priest described as "generous Indians, friendly to the point of giving whatever they had." Vizcaíno named the bay Monte Rey, in honor of the count of Monte Rey, viceroy of Mexico, who had sent him on his expedition.

Contact between California's native people and Europeans was sparse, though, until Spanish missionaries arrived in 1769, planning to convert the people they called Diggers to Christianity. (Priests gave them this name after watching native women dig up edible bulbs with pointed sticks.) The missionaries found a region inhabited by many different tribes, belonging to over a hundred language groups and speaking more than three hundred dialects.

California's rich natural environment provided its native people with everything they needed for a comfortable life, including the most varied diet on the continent. Most tribes used acorns as a staple food, but they could also fish, hunt wild game, and collect hundreds of edible plants. Natural materials for shelter were plentiful, too. People who lived along the coast built conical homes from redwood bark slabs. In the marshlands, their thatched shelters were made of tule, a reed like bulrush. The Kumeyaay, a desert people, shaded themselves under palm-frond *ramadas*, or porches, while the Hupa split cedar logs with stone hammers and elk-antler wedges to make more elaborate shelters.

*K*now that on the right hand of the Indies, there is an island called California, very near to the Terrestrial Paradise.

— From a Spanish romance novel, written in 1510

*Thatched Indian houses near the mission of San Luis Rey*

The Chumash and other native peoples made houses of earth and brush.

Women of all tribes were skilled basket makers.

In the region's warm climate, men wore little clothing. Women dressed in skirts made from tule or palm fronds. In the colder months, men and women wrapped themselves in animal skins.

In some tribes, such as the Hupa, women were the healers; in others, such as the Luiseño, the shamans were men. Native people measured their wealth in woodpecker scalps, rare white deerskins, dentalium beads (made from seashells), and in the intricate baskets woven by women of all tribes. As they fished in mountain rivers, they often found glittering gold nuggets embedded in the streambeds, but they ignored them. The gold stone was much too soft to be useful.

Because there was plenty of land and food to go around, most neighboring tribes lived without conflict. Coastal Indians—who had never seen horses, rarely went to war, and had no weapons to protect themselves against gunfire—were easily captured by the Spanish. Miwoks, Yokuts, Pomos, and Kumeyaays were seized and forced into missions along the coast. There, they were treated like slaves and weren't allowed to follow their former beliefs and ways of life.

One man who grew up under this system was a Miwok named José Jesús. Born in a mission and baptized with a Catholic name, Jesús struggled to survive as Spanish diseases killed many of his relatives. Mission cattle ruined Miwok grasslands and drove away the wild game. Missionaries separated husbands and wives and took children from their parents, beating and

*José Jesús was raised in a mission similar to this one at San Carlos, near Monterey.*

lashing those who disobeyed their rules. When Jesús was a young man, he escaped from his mission and became a raider, stealing livestock from his former captors.

*A Native American hunter*

In 1834, when Mexico became independent from Spain, missionaries were supposed to return their lands to native people. Instead, Mexican settlers seized Miwok, Pomo, and Yokut land for their *ranchos* and continued to keep Indians as laborers. Some native people, such as José Jesús, managed to avoid *rancho* life. But fifteen years after the missions closed, gold was discovered, and Jesús and other mission Indians soon found themselves caught up in a much larger foreign invasion.

Spanish missionaries were afraid of the native people who lived in the remote mountain valleys, so these Indians had little contact with Europeans until the gold discovery. Lucy Young, a Wailiki (or Wintu) Indian who was probably born about 1846, remembered life before the white people came: "In early days,"

*Yuroks, Hupas, and Karoks performed the White Deerskin Dance, a ten-day ceremony to renew the earth.*

Lucy said, "everywhere you travel, was good water." The Wailikis lived on black salmon, acorns, nuts, and wild berries. Small roasted grasshoppers were a delicacy. The women wove nets from the wild iris plant and used them to catch fish, squirrels, and small birds. The men were in charge of hunting and cooking large game. Lucy's father, an expert arrow maker, tested new arrows on his arm. If the stone cut his skin quickly, it was sharp enough.

*My grandpa say, "White Rabbit" — he mean white people — "gonta devour our grass, our seed, our living. We won't have nothing more, this world."*

— *Lucy Young*

The Wailikis had everything they needed, except salt. Each year, members of the tribe made a long journey to salt springs belonging to an enemy tribe, traveling during the full moon so they could gather the salt without being seen. After a week's journey on foot, the fastest men and women crept to the springs to gather the crusty salt, glittering in the moonlight.

This peaceful way of life had lasted for centuries, but Lucy's grandfather, a bent old man with "eyes like indigo," had a vision of the changes that would come to his people. As Lucy recalled: "My grandpa say: 'White Rabbit'—he mean white people—'gonta devour our grass, our seed, our living. We won't have nothing more, this world.' My grandpa say, 'gonta be big canoe, run around, carry white people's things. Those White Rabbit got lotsa everything.'"

Lucy's grandfather didn't live long enough to see the white man's "canoes," or wagons, rumble over the dry ground. Miners didn't invade Lucy's isolated region until late in the gold rush, when Lucy was about nine or ten. Other mountain tribes—especially Nisenan, Miwok, Yokut, Maidu, Patwin, and Wintu Indians—lived in the heart of the region where gold was found. Their lives were turned upside down within a few months of the discovery at Sutter's mill.

The other people most affected by the gold rush were the Californios, descendants of the original Spanish settlers, who were raising cattle on

A map of general tribal areas before European settlement. Although the map shows distinct territories, native groups often overlapped, and boundaries shifted over time.

15

former mission lands. A boy named Ignacio Villegas grew up on one of these *ranchos*, east of Monterey Bay.

The Villegas family moved from Mexico to California just before the gold rush began. Ignacio and his brothers and sisters rode into California on horseback, trotting beside their mother, who sat with the baby in a big two-wheeled *carreta*, or cart, drawn by oxen. Ignacio was eight years old.

Like other Californio boys and girls, Ignacio learned to ride when he was very young. "There were no roads to speak of, only trails, and…for many years horseback was the principal means of travel," Ignacio said.

The countryside was dangerous, and children had to know how to protect themselves. Once, two grizzlies chased Ignacio until he was sure he would be mauled to death. He set fire to the grass, as he had seen Native Americans do, and scrambled into a tree, where he sat for six hours, watching the grass burn while many animals fled. Ignacio escaped unharmed.

Like other rancheros, Ignacio's father employed both Native American and Mexican workers to raise cattle and barley. He also expected his chil-

*Vaqueros, America's first cowboys*

dren to help, and Ignacio was given adult jobs at an early age. He rode with his father's vaqueros, the first cowboys, to capture wild horses roaming the San Joaquin Valley. When he was only eleven, Ignacio's father sent him to San Francisco, an overnight trip on horseback and by stagecoach, to find a man who owed them money. One December, Ignacio walked forty miles to pick up the family's Christmas presents, which had come into Monterey by ship.

Ignacio loved to read. He wanted to continue with school when he was a teenager, but his father insisted he become a vaquero instead. Ignacio let his hair grow to his shoulders as other

*The modern boy . . . cannot realize what it is to be isolated in a wild country, fearful that every time he gets a mile away from home a wild steer or bear will chase him.*

— *Ignacio Villegas*

vaqueros did, grew a mustache, and spent his days riding the boundaries of the *rancho*, keeping stray cattle from wandering onto the neighbor's land.

Because *ranchos* were often fifty or sixty miles apart and because there were few books, newspapers, or other forms of entertainment, families would organize fiestas, as well as bullfights and rodeos, that lasted a week or more. Girls and boys played a game with *cascarones* — eggs whose

*The del Valles, a typical Californio family, at Rancho Camulos*

*María Domínguez and Caroline Pico, two Californio girls from prominent Los Angeles families*

insides were blown out, then filled with perfumed confetti. The girls chased the boys, breaking the eggs on the heads of their favorites.

Ignacio had a lot of freedom, but life was strict for Californio girls. They were expected to stay inside and do housework by the time they were thirteen. Sometimes their parents locked them in their rooms at night to protect them from the boys, who slept outside on covered porches. Boys might have a little education if there was a school nearby, but most girls weren't taught to read or write, and they often married at a young age.

The peaceful life on the *ranchos* changed as news of the gold discovery spread across the state. Many vaqueros, as well as their bosses, caught *la fiebre del oro*. They abandoned their *ranchos* and galloped off to the diggings to pan for gold, bringing their Native American workers along.

Like the Native Americans living in the mountains, Californios had no idea that they would soon be living in the middle of an enormous invasion. In the busy ports of Boston, New York, and New Orleans, thousands of gold seekers were saying good-bye to their families and waiting for passage on the first available ships headed for California. The world's biggest migration was already underway.

# The Argonauts

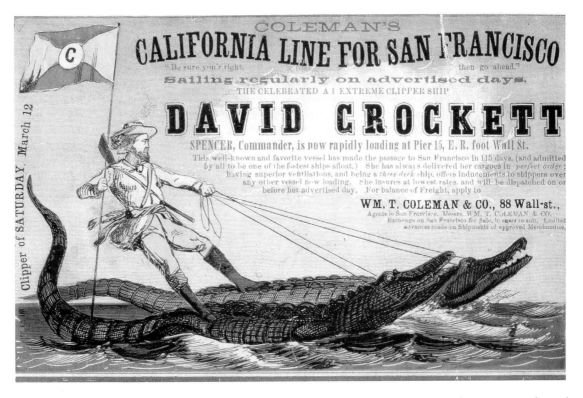

Within the advertisement:

COLEMAN'S
## CALIFORNIA LINE FOR SAN FRANCISCO
"Be sure you'r right,"     then go ahead."
**Sailing regularly on advertised days.**
THE CELEBRATED A 1 EXTREME CLIPPER SHIP
# DAVID CROCKETT
SPENCER, Commander, is now rapidly loading at Pier 15, E. R. foot Wall St.
This well-known and favorite vessel has made the passage to San Francisco in 115 days, (and admitted by all to be one of the fastest ships afloat,) She has always delivered her cargoes in *perfect order*; having superior ventilations, and being a *three deck* ship, offers inducements to shippers over any other vessel now loading. She insures at lowest rates, and will be dispatched on or before her advertised day. For balance of Freight, apply to
WM. T. COLEMAN & CO., 88 Wall-st.,
Agents in San Francisco, Messrs. WM. T. COLEMAN & CO.
Exchange on San Francisco for Sale, in sums to suit. Limited advances made on Shipments of approved Merchandise.

Clipper of SATURDAY, March 12

*Shipping companies hastened the spread of gold fever with ads such as this one.*

In the winter of 1849, New York State buzzed with talk about gold in California. Mifflin Gibbs was in Rochester, New York, with the great abolitionist Frederick Douglass, giving speeches against slavery. Their audiences were as cold as the weather outside, and Gibbs was worried about his future. Now that he had expressed such strong opinions on racial equality, it would be hard for him to find work, even though he was a skilled carpenter.

While Gibbs was in Rochester, he met a number of gold seekers, "many giving dazzling accounts of immense amounts of gold."

"Go do some great thing!" Gibbs told himself. Soon after, he booked passage in New York City on a steamer bound for San Francisco.

Dr. Thomas Megquier was also in New York, with his business partner, a druggist named Cyrus Richmond. Megquier (pronounced *meh-GWEER*)

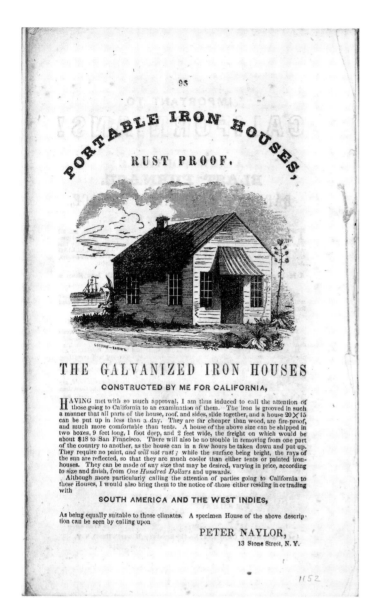

*An ad for a portable iron house similar to the house Dr. Thomas Megquier shipped around Cape Horn*

had given up his sluggish medical practice in Maine and was planning to move to the Sandwich Islands. His family would join him if his new practice proved successful. Thomas's wife, Mary Jane, known as Jennie, wished their three children Merry Christmas by mail and took the train to New York in a snowstorm to see her husband off.

New York's harbor was a tangle of masts. Docks were laden with supplies as stevedores loaded ships departing for the long journey around Cape Horn, the southernmost tip of South America, to California. Thomas Megquier changed his plans. San Francisco, Megquier told Jennie, needed physicians. What better way to bring home his own piece of the gold rush? Dr. Megquier and Cyrus Richmond bought a portable frame building called an iron house and arranged to have it shipped around Cape Horn.

Then Thomas surprised his wife by inviting her to join him. "It is so expensive getting women's work, they think it will pay well," Jennie wrote their daughter, Angeline, who was seventeen. "It won't be more than four or six months and all I want you to do is to make yourself and the boys comfortable anywhere you please."

When the Megquiers were swept up by the rush for gold, they didn't know that it would be two long years before they saw their children again. As for Mifflin Gibbs, he didn't return east until long after the Civil War had ended.

•◆•

California gold seekers chose between two methods of travel: land or sea. The men and women who traveled to California by boat during the gold rush were known as argonauts, after adventurers in Greek mythology who sailed with the hero Jason on his ship *Argo* in search of the Golden Fleece. For travelers such as Mifflin Gibbs and the Megquiers, eager to leave right away, a sea voyage was the only option in the winter. The overland trails would be impassable until the snow melted in the spring.

There were two main sea routes to California. The seventeen-thousand-mile trip around South America's Cape Horn took from five to seven months, and cost between one hundred and three hundred dollars. Steamship travel by way of Panama was much quicker (some companies promised to deliver the argonauts to San Francisco in thirty days, although that rarely happened), but more expensive: Tickets cost between two hundred and four hundred dollars.

*Jennie Megquier*

The Megquiers decided to send their house, medicines, and belongings by way of Cape Horn while they, Jennie wrote her daughter, would take "a small steamer to Chagres [Panama], where we shall change and take another up the Chagres River about 75 miles, then we take mules for 24 miles, then there is a large steamer for San Francisco which will take about 30 days if we have good luck.

*Bring your wife along, for a good wife is the scarcest article in California.*

— *Letter in the* NEW YORK HERALD

I have made me a double gown of red calico, a tunic and trousers for crossing the isthmus.... Your father has bought me a side saddle."

When Jennie boarded the steamer, she was the only woman among two hundred men. Her family claimed she was the first American woman to cross the Isthmus of Panama during the gold rush.

Although the isthmus route was quick, it had its disadvantages. Passengers had to pay for transportation across the isthmus and for lodging

*Mifflin Gibbs*

along the way. Because they had to move their baggage overland, they were warned not to carry more than 150 pounds of luggage. And many travelers taking the Panama route came down with tropical diseases.

The first argonauts embarked on crowded steamships from New York, Boston, or New Orleans, sometimes sleeping in cabins with fifteen other passengers, or even in lifeboats if the ships were overbooked. Mifflin Gibbs had no complaints about his journey, finding that "a common brotherhood tightens the chain of fellowship." But other African Americans found that racism was as common at sea as it was on land. They paid for third-class passage, only to be forced out of their bunks by white crew members who wanted a better bed.

After a few weeks at sea, the argonauts were left off in the village of Chagres, which Jennie described as "the most beautiful spot I ever saw. The shores are covered with a thick growth of trees and in front of us rises one of those old castles that we read of."

Like the Megquiers, Mifflin Gibbs had never been out of the United States. He enjoyed observing people who had come to Panama from all over the world, including some freed American slaves who had opened hotels and restaurants or operated the boats that carried travelers up the Chagres River.

African Americans often warned their fellow travelers to watch out for Panamanian kidnappers who would try to sell them back into slavery. Gibbs was more concerned about the tropical fever, which "stalked from conquest to conquest" and made him very sick.

Like most argonauts, the Megquiers went upriver in a bungo, "a canoe about two feet wide and twenty feet long with baggage enough to load a stout horse in our country," as Jennie described it to her daughter. "We were propelled along by two natives," she added, "one in the bow with a pole, the other in the stern with a paddle." Jennie Megquier was amazed by the sights along the way. "The air was filled with the music of the birds, the chattering of the monkeys, parrots in any quantity, alligators lying on the banks too lazy to move."

*The Megquiers and Mifflin Gibbs enjoyed the sights along the shores of the Chagres River.*

The Megquiers stayed in bamboo huts with wooden floors, where they choked down meals of grilled iguana and baked monkey. In these crude hotels, men and women who didn't know one another crowded into the same room. The artist J. Goldsborough Bruff woke up one morning "astonished to see a young woman sitting up also in the next cot...fastening her dress, while all around were upwards of a hundred men."

Argonauts made the last part of the trip on foot or on mules. Jennie Megquier decided that the trail was "one of the roughest roads in the world." Many women, used to riding sidesaddle in a skirt, put on pants and boots for the journey. Children were carried in hammocks or on the backs of their native guides. Everyone had to watch out for snakes and wild animals and for the treacherous mud on the heavily traveled track. Many came down with yellow fever, malaria, or dysentery.

Once they reached the Pacific side of the isthmus, the early argonauts faced another obstacle: there were not enough boats to bring them up the West Coast to San Francisco. While travelers waited for days or weeks for a steamship to carry them on the last leg of their journey, some died in the cholera epidemic that raged in Panama City. Gibbs took a berth on the *Golden Gate,* which had "a stormy passage, making San Diego with the top of the smokestack encrusted with the salt of the waves, [and] paddle wheel broken." He reached San Francisco in September.

*I should not grudge the expense at all if we did not make one cent, to see what we have seen.*

— *Jennie Megquier*

*Shipping companies lured passengers with promises of speedy passage.*

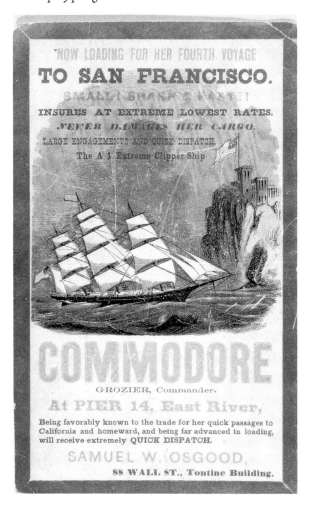

The argonauts who chose the Cape Horn route faced five to seven long months at sea. They paid less for their passage but had to contend with fierce storms, months of boredom, overcrowding, and scurvy, a disease caused by a lack of fresh fruits and vegetables. To amuse themselves, passengers played cards, sewed, put on plays, read books, wrote letters, sang, came up with practical jokes, gave scientific lectures, and tried to catch albatrosses, giant ocean birds with a wingspan of twelve feet.

Cholera broke out on many ships. Some boats caught fire or were shipwrecked. One woman, a Mrs. Bates, sailed on three different ships that caught fire! To escape the smoke and fumes on one boat, she tied herself to a chair on deck, where she was drenched by "sheets of foam, dashing over the bows, as the doomed ship plunged into the angry water."

*Argonauts traveling on clipper ships often experienced fierce storms.*

Storms were fierce as ships rounded Cape Horn. Elizabeth Gunn was traveling with her four children to California to meet her husband. It was hard to entertain the children on board their ship, the *Bengal,* and they ran into a gale. "We were tossed about in fine order," she wrote. "We could neither stand nor sit and of course must lie down.... The children sat against the side of the cabin, and held their plates in their laps, and

*You can't keep hold of your things ... and you can no more walk than you can fly.*

— *Elizabeth Gunn, describing her shipboard passage around Cape Horn*

half the time one would spill his water or lose his spoon.... You can't keep hold of your things ... and you can no more walk than you can fly."

No matter which sea route they chose, the argonauts all disembarked in San Francisco. They found a rough town becoming a city overnight. The harbor was filled with ships: clippers with towering masts, sturdy

*Ships stranded in
San Francisco's harbor
when their crews left
for the mines*

steamboats, and smaller yawls and ketches. There were no docks, so passengers climbed into smaller boats, then waded through deep mud to reach the shore.

Mifflin Gibbs stepped onto dry land with sixty cents in his pocket. He paid a man fifty cents to take his trunk to a boardinghouse, where the sign at the desk, in gilt letters, stated BOARD TWELVE DOLLARS A WEEK IN ADVANCE. Gibbs had no idea how he would earn his board, but he had been working full-time ever since his father died, when he was eight years old. Something would come up. Without hesitating, he spent his last dime on a cigar.

*It is the most God-forsaken country in the world.*

— *Jennie Megquier, describing San Francisco*

Weary travelers were lucky to have any shelter at all. To build a house, Jennie Megquier told her daughter, people "put up a few joists and cover it over with cotton cloth." When ships' crews abandoned their boats for the goldfields, some emigrants got back on board and converted the empty

26

ships into crude houses or hotels. One enterprising woman kept a dairy cow on her ship and sold precious cream, as well as hand-churned butter, from the deck. Jennie Megquier opened a boardinghouse while her husband started his medical practice.

There was no place to store the cargo being unloaded from the ships; Jennie watched "carts running over bags of flour and rice, and hard bread." And when the fall rains came, the streets were nearly impassable with sticky mud. Food was scarce, and fresh vegetables cost a fortune. The most common entertainment took place in the gambling halls, where men could lose all their earnings in just a few hours.

Jennie Megquier was surprised by the way people dressed: "The greatest dandies wear their beard long, their hair uncombed, a very dirty colored shirt, and coarse jacket, their skin brown from the sun and dust." San Francisco was the "City of Dust," she wrote to her cousins, referring both to the dust that blew with the constant winds and the golden dust that lured people west by the thousands. "It is the most God-forsaken country in the world," she concluded.

Many other argonauts sent similar warnings to gold seekers back East, but it was too late. Spring had come to the Great Plains, and enormous caravans were gathering in Missouri. Like racehorses ready to bolt from the starting gate, thousands of restless emigrants waited for the rains to stop, each party determined to be the first to reach the diggings.

*Jennie Megquier (second from right) on a visit home to see a new grandchild*

# The Overland Trail

*Wagons and tents on the prairie, drawn into a circle for the night*

*Margaret Frink*

**A**bout the same time that argonauts like the Megquiers reached San Francisco, thousands of gold seekers were gathering on the banks of the Missouri River, packed tightly into campgrounds that sprawled out around St. Joseph and Independence, Missouri, the most popular jumping-off places for the overland journey. Their red-gold campfires lit the night sky for miles.

The overland gold seekers called themselves emigrants, because they were leaving the settled United States behind. Among this group was young Sallie Hester, traveling with her parents, brothers, and sister; and Margaret Frink, who had set out from Indiana with her eleven-year-old foster son, Robert Parker, and her husband, Ledyard.

Most emigrants were young white men, but some were women; a few, like Sallie Hester, were children. Some emigrants were African Americans eager to reach California because it planned to enter the union as a free state. Other were foreigners, such as Hermann J. Sharmann, a young German who had traveled from Brooklyn, New York, with his parents, brother, and young sister.

As they waited for the spring rains to stop and the grass to green up for their animals, the Sharmanns, like the Frinks and the Hesters, used the extra time to organize themselves into traveling companies. Hermann Sharmann's father was elected captain of a train of seventy-five emigrants. The Sharmanns had a tough decision to make: Should they buy oxen or mules to haul their wagons? Mules were faster, and they made good sentinels, braying loudly if a stranger or a wild animal approached the camp at night. But they were more expensive and spooked easily. Oxen were stronger and could travel farther without water. Plus, travelers could eat them if they ran out of other food. The Sharmanns, like the majority of emigrants, settled on oxen.

*1849 will ever be a memorable epoch in the history of our country. Neither the crusades nor Alexander's expedition to India . . . can equal this emigration to California.* — Dr. C. N. Omsby, July 24, 1849

*A large Mormon family headed west*

While they were waiting, the emigrants bought food and supplies for the half year they would spend living and traveling in their sturdy covered wagons. They visited groceries, blacksmiths, gunsmiths, and saddler's shops.

The Hester family's wagons were loaded with "a cooking stove made of sheet iron, a portable table, tin plates and cups, cheap knives and forks."

*St. Joe, April 27, 1849. As far as eye can reach, so great is the emigration, you see nothing but wagons.*

*— Sallie Hester*

They had brought their own cows, and in St. Joseph, the Hesters stocked up on "bacon, ham, rice, dried fruits, molasses, packed butter, bread, coffee, tea." Overland travelers also packed tools for mining, farming, and repairing the wagons; vegetable and flower seeds; medicines, guns, and ammunition; awls, needles, and strong thread for mending clothes and tents; and bedding, including buffalo robes.

Everything had to fit in a wagon nine feet long and four or five feet wide. The wagon was covered with canvas or a heavy cotton fabric called

*A covered wagon was a home on wheels.*

*Thousands of emigrants and their animals competed for fresh water and scarce food.*

osnaburg, which was waterproofed with linseed oil. The cover was held up by five hickory hoops. Travelers carried waterproof india rubber blankets to help keep things dry and lock-chains to hold their wagons back on steep hills. Some even brought chickens, swinging from a cage at the back of the wagon.

Although many travelers chose the overland route because they thought it would cost less than going by sea, most families of four spent between six and seven hundred dollars to outfit themselves for the journey.

The first part of the trip was usually the easiest as well as the most pleasant. "This is a beautiful spot," Sallie Hester wrote. "The Plains are covered with flowers." There was plenty of water and grass for the animals, and lots of wild game. Helen Carpenter, a young woman traveling with her new husband, described the scene after a buffalo

*For weeks we plodded on and on into a world that was a brown flat plate under an inverted blue cup.*

— *Hermann J. Sharmann*

hunt: "Tonight the wagons are decorated with slices of meat dangling from strings . . . looking very much like coarse red fringe."

Many emigrants came from towns and cities and were not used to the rough life on the trail. Sallie Hester's overweight mother had to be "lifted in and out of our wagons in St. Joe." But after a few weeks on the trail, Sally wrote in her diary that "Mother now walks a mile or two without stopping, and gets in and out of the wagons as spry as a young girl."

As they left the more settled parts of the country, travelers worried about attacks by Sioux and other Plains Indians. Margaret Frink found them "quite friendly. The squaws were much pleased to see the 'white squaw' in our party, as they called me." Frink traded needles, thread, and small mirrors to the Sioux for fresh antelope, deer, and buffalo meat, while her foster son, Robert Parker, was thrilled to find a Sioux willing to exchange deerskin moccasins for his tight leather shoes. Emigrants soon learned they were much more likely to shoot each other by accident, to drown while crossing a swollen river, or to die from diseases than to be killed by Native Americans.

Most companies traveled fifteen or twenty miles a day. Everyone in the family had to work hard to make sure they didn't get left behind. One of their most difficult jobs was lowering a heavy wagon down a steep hill.

*Bringing a wagon train down a long hill*

*Supper on the trail, complete with a tablecloth*

Margaret Frink and young Robert chocked the wheels with stones or blocks of wood to keep the wagons from hurtling forward while the men held the oxen or mules back with lock-chains. They also divided other chores: Robert learned to cook and helped Margaret with the washing. When feed for the animals ran low, Margaret and Robert tied blades of sparse grass into bundles while Ledyard drove the oxen.

Most emigrants found it hard to stick by the rules they had followed back home. If a woman's long skirt grew short after many scorchings by the fire, she might leave it that way. She could even shock her traveling companions by wearing bloomers, loose pants worn under a medium-length skirt, which made it easier to climb in and out of the wagon, wrestle with a stubborn mule, or haul water from the Platte River.

The trip could be difficult for children. Those who had grown up in small towns or cities were afraid of the night sounds: wolves howling and panthers screeching beyond the circle of wagons. Some feared the vast emptiness of the prairie. Worst of all was the secret killer the overland companies had brought with them from the east: a cholera epidemic that

struck many children as well as their parents. Hermann Sharmann's mother and sister both got sick; his sister died, and Hermann wrote, sadly, "I have never been able to identify the spot."

Children also fell out of wagons and were sometimes crushed under the wheels. Some were separated from their parents at busy river crossings, while others drowned. Children might be orphaned on the trail and taken in by strangers. Dying children begged their parents to pile rocks over their graves to protect their bodies from wolves. Funeral services were brief; the rush continued westward, and stragglers would be left behind.

But children also enjoyed the excitement of the journey—the chance to hunt buffalo and antelope, to pick wildflowers and play games as the wagons rolled slowly along, or to paint their initials on famous landmarks, using a mixture of gunpowder and bacon grease. Sallie Hester was excited when she carved her name on Independence Rock (so-called because travelers often reached it around Independence Day). Robert Parker and his mother delighted in their summer snowball fight at Willow Springs.

*Thousands of emigrants carved their names on Independence Rock.*

Sometimes children's curiosity got them into trouble. Where the Sweetwater River cut through a canyon called Devils Gate, Sallie Hester and some other children went exploring. "We made our way to the very edge of the cliff and looked down," Sallie wrote. "We could hear the water dashing, splashing and roaring as if angry at the small space through which it was forced to pass. We were gone so long that the train was stopped and men sent out in search of us. We made all sorts of promises to remain in sight in the future."

Like children everywhere, the young emigrants had jobs to do. If they had grown up on a farm, they were used to caring for animals, hauling water, helping with younger children, or cooking. But hunting buffalo, driving a team of oxen, gathering wild edible plants, or collecting buffalo chips (dried manure) for the fire were new experiences.

> *We were gone so long that the train was stopped and men sent out in search of us. We made all sorts of promises to remain in sight in the future.*
>
> — *Sallie Hester*

As the trail wound along beside the Platte River, the journey became more difficult. The first year of the migration, 1849, was one of the rainiest years on records. Frightening hailstorms drenched the wagon trains. Rivers, swollen from the spring rains, swept men and oxen downstream during crossings. Some wagons were mired in mud or quicksand; others smashed in the current. Emigrants caught dysentery from dirty drinking water. Some gave up and turned around, heading back east with their heads down.

But the lure of gold kept most pushing ahead, even though the trip grew harder as the Rocky Mountains loomed at the edge of the prairie. Oxen and mules died from eating bad grass or from hauling heavy loads. To ease the weight, emigrants dumped furniture, food, stoves, and tools beside the road. The wagon trains found a smooth cut through the Rock-

*Emigrants forded many rivers during the journey west.*

Even young children helped
with chores, including hunting
for small game.

ies at South Pass, but from then on the trip became even more dangerous. "Roads are rocky and trying to our wagons, and the dust is horrible," Sallie wrote. "The men wear veils tied over their hats as a protection. When we reach camp at night, they are covered with dust from head to heels."

By late summer or early fall, the emigrants were following Nevada's Humboldt River, a strange, muddy current that doesn't flow out to the sea but is swallowed up in a barren valley known as the Humboldt Basin. Beyond the basin lay the dreaded Forty-Mile Desert. The pioneers had heard terrible stories about the desert crossing: the lack of food and water, the scorching heat, and the deep sand that mired the oxen. Most of all, emigrants feared attacks from the native people of the regions, known as the Diggers. The fierce Diggers, it was rumored, might raid their campgrounds at night, steal their food and animals, and poison their water. Who were these people, so different from the Native Americans they had seen on the plains?

# The Great American Desert

**W**hen Thocmetony, a Numa (or Paiute) Indian, was a little girl, her grandfather, Chief Winnemucca, told her a story. Once a family had four children: a dark-skinned boy and girl and a light-skinned boy and girl. The dark and light children couldn't get along, so their parents sent them to live apart. The dark boy and girl grew into the nations of Indian people, while the pale boy and girl started the nations of whites. One day, the legend promised, the white nation would send messengers to the dark nation to heal the troubles between them.

Soon after Thocmetony heard this story, some strangers arrived in the Humboldt Desert Basin, where the Numas lived. Thocmetony's father called the people "owl-faced men," because hair grew on their faces and their eyes were as pale as the great night bird. But Chief Winnemucca believed that they were the special messengers from the legend, so he helped them find their way across the desert and over the Sierra Nevada, the mountain range to the west. The leader of the owl-faced men, John Charles Frémont, liked Chief Winnemucca so much that he called him Captain Truckee, after the Numa word for "very good."

When he came home from California, Chief Winnemucca told Thocmetony about the strange houses of the owl-faced men. Some could travel on the water. Others moved on the ground. And these men had a gun that could shoot a ball as big as Thocmetony's head.

Even though she loved and trusted her grandfather, Thocmetony was terrified of the owl-faced men. She had heard different stories about them from the Numa women. Her mother and aunt had told Thocmetony that the white people killed Numa children and ate them.

On a hot fall morning in 1847, when Thocmetony was three, her mother and sister were gathering seeds near the Humboldt River. Hearing that some owl-faced men were coming, the women gathered their children and ran away. Thocmetony and her little cousin couldn't run fast enough, so their mothers buried them in sand, covering their faces with sagebrush to keep out the sun, and told them to lie still and not make a sound.

*Thocmetony*
*(Sarah Winnemucca)*

Thocmetony and her cousin stayed buried all day, listening to lizards, mice, and scorpions scuttling through the sand. Finally their mothers rescued them, but the owl-faced men had burned the grass and mud mounds where the Numa women had stored their food for the winter.

*I was a very small child when the first white people came into our country. They came like a lion…
and have continued so ever since, and I have never forgotten their first coming.*

— Thocmetony (Sarah Winnemucca)

In 1849, thousands of owl-faced men, women, and children streamed through Numa land, traveling in the moving homes Winnemucca had described. Thocmetony's family fled, but they heard how the white men burned more of their winter food supplies and shot some of the Numa who had stayed behind.

The next year, some owl-faced men shot Thocmetony's uncle and five other Numas. Her mother and aunt cut off their hair and gashed their

Paiute leaders (left to right) Thocmetony (Sarah Winnemucca); her father, Chief Winnemucca; her brother, Chief Natchez; and another Paiute known as Captain Jim

arms and legs, which was the custom when relatives died. Numa warriors wanted revenge, but Chief Winnemucca wouldn't allow them to kill the people he still thought of as his "white brothers," even though they had murdered his son.

Chief Winnemucca heard that the owl-faced men had found a precious stone in the rivers of California. He decided he would take Thocmetony and thirty other families over the Sierras to learn the ways of the white people. Thocmetony was horrified. How could her beloved grandfather force her to live among the people who had caused so much suffering?

Thocmetony spent the winter on a ranch, where she learned to eat sugar, to use a knife and fork, to wear a dress, and to speak English. She was also given an English name: Sarah. It didn't have the same special sound as Thocmetony, which meant Shellflower, but it was a name she would carry with her for the rest of her life.

When Thocmetony and her relatives returned to the Great Basin in the spring, they discovered that hundreds of Numas had died from a disease brought by the white settlers. Thocmetony didn't understand. Some of the owl-faced people had been kind to her. One white woman in California had bathed her eyes when they were swollen shut from poison oak. Why did other whites want to kill her friends and relatives?

To the Numas, the desert was home, a place of harsh beauty. To owl-faced people such as the Hesters, the Sharmanns, and the Frinks, crossing the Forty-Mile Desert was a nightmare. Emigrants ran out of food and water. Their oxen died. "The dead animals...lay so thick on the ground that the carcasses, if placed together, would have reached across many miles of that desert. The stench arising was continuous and terrible," Margaret Frink wrote.

*The dead animals...lay so thick on the ground that the carcasses, if placed together, would have reached across many miles of that desert. The stench arising was continuous and terrible.*
— Margaret Frink

The final obstacle was the most difficult: crossing the Sierra Nevada. Some travelers cut their wagons in half or burned them for fuel, packing the last of their possessions on their animals' backs for the rocky ascent.

*After crossing the Forty-Mile Desert, emigrants faced one last obstacle: the rugged Sierra Nevada.*

Still others, such as an African-American woman whom Margaret Frink saw, made the final journey on foot. The woman "came tramping along through the heat and dust, carrying a cast-iron bake oven on her head, with her provisions and blankets piled on top," Frink wrote.

Sallie Hester's family reached the Sierras in September. They traveled through the night, and Sallie never forgot "our tedious march with pine knots blazing in the darkness and the tall, majestic pines towering above our heads." For days, they inched up the steep mountains, edging their way around giant gray boulders, then lowering the wagons slowly down the other side.

While the Hesters and Frinks struggled to cross the Sierras before snow fell, the Brier family had just arrived in Salt Lake City, more than five hundred miles behind. Kirk Brier was nine years old, the oldest of three brothers. His mother, Juliette, was thirty-five and frail. His father, James, a Methodist minister, was not well either. It was October, far too late to start out across the desert and the final range of mountains into

California. Instead, the Briers joined with one hundred wagons, under the leadership of Jefferson Hunt, who had agreed to lead them on the Old Spanish Trail to Los Angeles.

*E*very step I expected to sink down and die.

— *Juliette Brier*

The southern routes were not as popular or as well known as the California Trail. Emigrants wound through dry territory recently owned by Mexico, where water and grass were scarce, and crossed the country of the Apaches, feared because of exaggerated rumors about their cruelty toward people who trespassed on their land.

About nine thousand emigrants chose the southern routes in 1849. Some enjoyed the trails through Arizona and New Mexico because there were frequent towns and trading posts, where they could buy fresh produce and feed for their animals. Although many complained about the endless miles of sagebrush and the thick dust, others marveled at the sight of giant saguaro cactus and at the impressive views of cliffs and mountain ranges that turned a rosy pink in the sunset.

Unfortunately the Briers would not have pleasant memories. A few days out of Salt Lake City, their company ran into a pack train led by a guide named O.K. Smith. Smith claimed that a nearby cutoff would shorten their desert trip by six hundred miles. Kirk's father was eager to try this alternate route, which he hoped would be easier on Juliette and the boys.

Captain Hunt knew the dangers of unmarked trails, but some of the emigrants, including the Briers, were determined to try the so-called shortcut. They

*Juliette Brier, her husband, James, and their three sons, who barely survived the desert now known as Death Valley*

broke away from the rest of the train, taking twenty-seven wagons and calling themselves the Jayhawkers.

Before long, they entered the desert that local Indians called Tomesha, or "ground afire." The Briers burned their wagon and loaded the last of their possessions onto their oxen. When they reached Furnace Creek, Kirk Brier broke down. Years later, Juliette still remembered his pleading cries: "'Oh, Father, where's the water?' His pitiful, delirious wails were worse to hear than the killing thirst. It was terrible.... I staggered and struggled wearily behind the other two boys and the oxen.... Every step I expected to sink down and die."

*You will hardly find a family that has not left some beloved one buried upon the plains.*

— *Dame Shirley*

Some of the Jayhawkers, watching Juliette carry one son on her back and another in her arms, while holding the third by the hand, suggested she stay behind until they could send someone to rescue her, but she refused. "I knew what that meant: a shallow grave in the sand."

Members of the party began to die of thirst and exhaustion. The Reverend Brier, who had lost one hundred pounds, couldn't stand up unless Juliette helped him to his feet. She made him a tiny meal of ground acorns, and he staggered on. "Night came down," Juliette remembered, "and we lost all track of those ahead. I would get down on my knees and look in the starlight for the ox tracks." They traveled for forty-eight hours without water, finally discovering a spring on Christmas morning. Two months later, they came upon a herd of cattle belonging to a Mexican rancher. The Briers were saved. "It was like coming back from death into life again," Juliette Brier said.

Six to eight months after they left Missouri, the gold seekers finally reached the diggings. Louise Clappe, who wrote articles about the gold rush under the pen name Dame Shirley, described the worn emigrants who stumbled into her mining camp that winter and spring of 1850: "The poor women arrive, looking as haggard as so many Endorean witches; burnt to the color of a hazel-nut, with their hair cut short, and its gloss

*At the end of their long journey, emigrants stopped at California way stations to buy supplies before heading for the diggings.*

entirely destroyed by the alkali.... You will hardly find a family that has not left some beloved one buried upon the plains."

Hermann Sharmann, looking back on the journey, wrote, "Young as I was at the time, the terrible sufferings and privations we endured have never been effaced from my mind."

# In the Diggings

*Panning for gold, the simplest, most common method in the early days*

The English prospector J.D. Borthwick arrived in California on a hot summer day. He traveled from Sacramento to the diggings by stagecoach, wearing his "worst clothes" and carrying only a roll of blankets, a sketch pad and charcoal, and his pipe. He was impressed by the view as the stage rattled across "an ocean of grass-covered earth." But he was dismayed when he reached Hangtown, a camp with one long, winding street "strewed with old boots, hats, shirts, old sardine-boxes, empty tins of preserved oysters, empty bottles, worn-out pots and kettles...and other rubbish."

Like thousands of other gold seekers, Borthwick had expected to find rivers overflowing with gold. He was in for a shock. "Men used to pick chunks of gold out of crevices...with no other tool than a bowie knife, but those days are gone," he wrote sadly. Crowds of miners lined the rivers and stream banks. They were digging in the middle of the street, even under the floors of houses. "There was a continual noise and clatter, as mud, dirt, stones, and water were thrown about in all directions." Striking it rich would not be easy.

*Men used to pick chunks of gold out of crevices… with no other tool than a bowie knife, but those days are gone.*

—*J.D. Borthwick*

Borthwick was an artist and writer; his fellow prospectors had been storekeepers, laborers, teachers, seamstresses, farmers. They knew little about mining and had to learn from Sonorans, who had arrived early from Mexico, or from Native Americans. These more experienced miners taught the newcomers that gold usually occurs in veins in bedrock. Moving water eats away at the rock, loosens the gold, and carries it down-

*Rough mining camps sprang up overnight.*

*A miner's most important tools were his pick and shovel.*

stream. California's frequent earthquakes also shift the bedrock over time and bring it to the surface, exposing the gold. Gold is heavier than sand and gravel, so it settles and sinks to the bottom as it travels downstream. The miners searched for gold at bends in the stream or other places where the current moved more slowly. Only the lucky ones found loose nuggets gleaming in the streambed.

To stake a claim, Borthwick and his partners simply set their picks and shovels on a promising piece of ground outside town and moved into an abandoned cabin nearby. Their tools were simple: pickaxes to break up the rock, shovels to move earth and stone, and gold pans.

Placer mining, the process of washing soil and gravel to find gold, was hard work. The dry days of summer and early fall were best for mining because the rivers were low, exposing stony areas where gold might be hiding. But the heat was intense. Writing in his diary, Borthwick recorded working in temperatures as high as 120 degrees. Borthwick and other miners waded into the icy river, scooped a mix of stones, sand, and gravel into their pans, and held them underwater while they poured off the big stones. Then they stirred the muddy mixture in the pans with one hand, letting more gravel slide out. Finally they swirled the pans around and around, letting fresh water in as the loosened gravel floated out.

At the end of the day, Borthwick and his partners washed the final gleanings from the Long Tom, then set their pans by a fire to dry the last bits of sediment. The Sonorans used their wool serapes to winnow the gold from the sand, stretching the ponchos tight and bouncing them gently. The wind blew the dried sand away while the gold dust settled on the wool.

*There was a continual noise and clatter, as mud, dirt, stones, and water were thrown in all directions.*

— J.D. Borthwick

It was hard work, but anyone who was strong and determined could pan for gold. Although most miners were men, a few women also tried their luck. Dame Shirley was "sorry she learned the trade" after her first attempt at panning: "I wet my feet, tore my dress, spoilt a pair of new

*A miner rocking a cradle. The miner shoveled water and gravel into the sluice box, then rocked the cradle to separate gold from the sediment.*

Men and women had to
haul water from the rivers
for daily chores such as
cooking and washing.

gloves, nearly froze my fingers, got an awful headache, took cold and lost a valuable breast-pin, in this my labor of love."

Mary Ballou, who tried mining before she opened a boardinghouse, rocked a heavy mining cradle all day to separate gold from the sediment. "I think it harder to wash out gold than it is to rock the cradle for the babies in the States," Ballou said.

*I have become a mineress; that is, if the having washed a pan of dirt with my own hands, and procured therefrom three dollars and twenty-five cents in gold dust… will entitle me to the name.*

— *Dame Shirley*

A small number of African Americans had early success in the mines. A black cook named Hector deserted his ship in Monterey, headed for the diggings, and returned with four thousand dollars in his pocket. Two African Americans made a lucky strike near Sutter's mill. Their settlement was known as Negro Hill and soon attracted other blacks, as well as Chinese and Portuguese miners. In the early months of the gold rush, black and white miners from the northern states worked side by side. Albert Callis, a freed slave, went into partnership with a white man named Downie, who later founded the town of Downieville. Callis mined as long as the claim yielded gold, then set up a barbershop in the growing settlement.

Black or white; Mexican, Chinese, or Irish; male or female—most miners were dismayed by how long it took to separate gold from sand, gravel, and mud.

•◆•

In the early days of the gold rush, blacks and whites worked side by side. Here, two men operate a Long Tom.

*When the journey was over, the Conestoga wagon could be converted into a spare room.*

As the fall rains sluiced down on the camps, the rivers rose, slowing the progress of mining. How would the emigrants survive the winter?

The Sharmann family's first Christmas in the mines was typical of that of many new arrivals. After nine months in their covered wagon, Hermann's father set up a crude shelter next to the two tents that made up the entire settlement of Bidwell's Bar. "The nearest town," Hermann remembered, "was Marysville, ninety miles away. We had no neighbors, and my mother was the only woman for many miles around in that wilderness.... By day, my father, my brother, and myself worked at placer mining on the Upper Feather River."

*Gold mining is Nature's Great Lottery Scheme.*

— *Dame Shirley*

Christmas was coming. Hermann was worried about his parents. They were still mourning their daughter, who had died crossing the plains. Like other miners who hadn't eaten fresh fruit or vegetables in months, Mr. and Mrs. Sharmann suffered from scurvy. What could Hermann and his brother, Jacob, do to cheer them up?

The boys saved ten dollars' worth of gold dust and rode the family horse to Marysville, where they spent all their earnings on a single can of peaches. Back at home, they prepared a feast of pancakes and biscuits with the last of their flour. While their parents watched from their pallets, Jacob carried the precious can to the "table" (a box on the floor), "bearing the peaches like a butler bringing the wassail bowl."

But their parents were too weak to touch their special treat, which spoiled the boys' excitement—and their appetite. Years later, when he was an old man, Hermann still remembered "our sad celebration under the canvas roof on the banks of the Upper Feather River."

Life in the diggings was just as difficult for other miners. As he moved from one claim to another, J.D. Borthwick lived in a lean-to made of brush, a tent that leaked, a cabin with a roof made of canvas, and another with a clapboard bed. Spending a night on that bed, Borthwick wrote, was "like sleeping on a gridiron." Window glass was rare; to let weak light

*J.D. Borthwick's sketch of his camp on Weaver Creek*

into their cabins, some miners cut the flat ends from glass jars, set them on end, and chinked them with mud.

Borthwick and his friends were able to buy a good supply of dried beef before the fall rains began. Other miners weren't so lucky. The steep mountain trails soon became slick with mud, making it difficult for mule trains to bring food into the more remote camps. Prices for the few available items became outrageously high. William Swain, a miner from New York State, wrote to his wife, Sabrina, that merchants were charging a dollar a pound for potatoes (which Sabrina could buy for half a cent per pound) and two dollars a pound for dried apples, which cost only four cents at home.

*Barbers were scarce, so many miners wore long hair and beards.*

Sanitary conditions were terrible in the camps. Livery stables shoveled horse manure straight into the muddy streets, where dead animals were left to rot and loose pigs rooted for food. Miners had no place to wash themselves or their clothes. Most men gave up shaving and let their hair grow long.

One in five miners died. Some drowned as the rivers flooded; others caught cholera or other diseases. Like many miners, William Swain suffered from rheumatism, a painful swelling in the joints caused by standing for long hours in cold water. To ease the pain, some miners lay on the riverbanks and buried their legs in hot sand to warm them. Swain instructed his brother, George, back East,

*A flume and paddle wheel diverted water from the riverbed.*

not to think of coming to the diggings, warning that "this mining among the mountains is a dog's life."

Swain was one of thousands of prospectors who quit the mines after his first hard winter. J.D. Borthwick also had bad luck in the diggings, but he discovered there were better ways to earn money. He liked to sketch miners and mining scenes during his lunch hour. People admired his drawings, and soon "every man wanted a sketch of his claim, or his cabin...and they all offered to pay very handsomely. I was satisfied that I could make paper and pencil much more profitable tools to work with than pick and shovel."

*This mining among the mountains is a dog's life.*

— William Swain

Borthwick had discovered the great secret of the gold rush. Like many other gold seekers, he quickly he threw "mining to the dogs" and filled his pockets using the talents he had brought with him from home.

# The Other Gold Rush

*R. Lowe's mining store advertised a "large supply kept constantly on hand."*

**T**housands of gold seekers arrived in California unprepared for the difficult life in the diggings. The men and women who provided them with tools, building supplies, groceries, and newspapers could earn a fortune: Sam Brannan made more than two thousand dollars a day at the store he built next to Sutter's Fort. Homesick miners also paid good money for the comforts of home: a hot meal, clean clothes, and a place to sleep at night.

The Villegas family's *rancho* in San Felipe sat next to the popular route for prospectors arriving from Sonora. Ignacio's parents took advantage of their location and opened a store and a restaurant that served twenty people at a time. With few trees or cut lumber available, they stretched wet cowhides over a crude frame to make the restaurant's walls. The family hunted wild game and served it to travelers for fifty cents a meal. If anyone complained, Ignacio wrote, "all they had to do was to travel to the next restaurant, which was several days farther on."

Getting supplies to remote camps was a challenge. Goods arrived in San Francisco by ship. From there, they were loaded onto smaller boats and carried up the river to Sacramento. Beyond Sacramento, rough roads deteriorated into trails, too narrow for a wagon or stagecoach. The best way to move supplies from

*Everyone must do something; it matters but very little what it is; if they stick to it, they are bound to make money.*

— Jennie Megquier

this point was on mules. The mule trains were often driven by Mexicans, referred to as *arrieros*. They tied bells to the animals' bridles, and miners dropped everything when they heard the distant jingle as the mules descended the sides of a steep ravine to the narrow valley floor. The *arrieros* brought tools, fresh food, and building supplies as well as the one thing emigrants missed more than anything else: news from home. Merchants charged $2.50 for each letter delivered and $1.50 for a newspaper

*Mules hauling heavy supplies didn't always cooperate with their arrieros, or mule drivers.*

*Miners exchanged gold dust for cash at the cash store.*

that cost only a nickel in the East. The letters and papers were six months out of date, but the miners read them eagerly.

Many of the men in the diggings had worked as carpenters, bricklayers, lawyers, doctors, storekeepers, newspaper editors, sailors, loggers, or boatbuilders before they came to California. After a few discouraging months in the mines or a long winter stuck in a damp cabin with no way to earn a living, many decided to use the skills they had brought with them. They abandoned the cold streams and built houses, took care of sick people, practiced law, sold groceries, or started newspapers. J.D. Borthwick traveled from one mining camp to another, selling his drawings of miners resting under the trees, gambling in saloons, or working in the rivers.

*I was satisfied that I could make paper and pencil much more profitable tools to work with than pick and shovel.*
— *J.D. Borthwick*

58

A few men started businesses that made them into household names. A man named Levi Strauss arrived in California with bolts of heavy canvas that he planned to make into tents. When he met a miner who needed strong, sturdy pants, he cut up the canvas and made him a pair. Other miners soon demanded "those pants of Levi's." Now his jeans are sold all over the world.

Another man, John Studebaker, built wheelbarrows for the miners until he earned enough money to return to his home state of Indiana, where he became the biggest wagon manufacturer in the country. Years later, when the automobile was invented, Studebaker wagons were replaced by Studebaker cars.

African Americans who had worked in the shipping industry around New Bedford, Massachusetts, found jobs on the steamboats that churned up the river to Sacramento. Those who had experience as cooks opened restaurants in the mines. One of the best known was called the Negro Tent, at Foster's Bar; it kept its original name even after its owner put up a frame building. African Americans opened barbershops or worked as cobblers as they had in the northern states. They were also in demand as bell ringers, who called out the news or advertised upcoming events in towns without newspapers.

*Levi Strauss*

The few women in the diggings discovered that their skills were invaluable. Most miners agreed with a man who complained that "in sewing, cooking, and washing I must confess myself at fault." Any woman willing

Hornblower's Store, like many in the mines, sold groceries, cigars, liquor, tools, and other supplies.

to cook, sew, or wash clothes for money could start collecting gold dust before she unpacked her bags.

One warm night in September of 1849, Luzena Stanley Wilson stood over an open fire near the booming town of Sacramento, making biscuits for her family. They had just finished the overland journey. When a stranger approached, she was embarrassed by the way she looked: "My skirts were torn off in rags above my ankles; my sleeves hung in tatters above my elbows; my hands, brown and hard, were gloveless...the soles of my leather shoes had long since parted company with the uppers." The man didn't care. He had smelled the sweet scent of fresh bread baking. "I'll give you five dollars, ma'am, for them biscuits," he said.

Luzena couldn't speak. How could a simple baking powder biscuit be worth so much money?

*In my dreams that night I saw crowds of bearded miners striking gold from the earth with every blow of the pick, each one seeming to leave a share for me.*

— *Luzena Stanley Wilson*

The miner must have thought he hadn't offered enough, because he held out a brand-new ten dollar gold piece.

In that moment, Luzena Wilson, like other men and women in the mines, caught a bad case of gold fever without ever touching a gold pan.

The next morning, "campfires crackled, breakfast steamed, and long lines of mules and horses, packed with provisions, filed past." Luzena and her husband were eager to begin earning money. They moved into town, sold their oxen for six hundred dollars, and bought an interest in a hotel.

The hotel was a success, but disaster struck that first winter. Rains pelted down, flooding the town. The Wilsons, stranded for seventeen days on the second floor of the hotel, lost a thousand dollars worth of barley, which sprouted when it got wet. "Ruin stared us in the face," Luzena remembered. Undaunted, she borrowed money to move her family to higher ground in Nevada City, where she set up her stove under a pine tree. She noticed a sign nearby, in front of a canvas shelter, reading WAMAC'S HOTEL. MEALS $1.00. Luzena decided to open a rival restaurant:

*The Louisiana Hotel in Jackson, California, was similar to the hotel operated by Luzena Wilson.*

"So I bought two boards from a precious pile.... With my own hands I chopped stakes, drove them into the ground, and set up my table.... I called my hotel 'El Dorado.'"

Before long, Luzena's business was thriving. She repaid her loan and made her husband a partner. Soon she was earning enough to hire a cook and waiters. Luzena also became a banker, lining her mattresses with gold dust and lending money at high rates of interest.

*Many a night have I shut my oven door on two milk-pans filled high with bags of gold dust.*

— Luzena Stanley Wilson

A year later, she lost her second hotel in a fire that destroyed most of Nevada City's main street. The Wilsons moved once more, to a fertile valley where Mr. Wilson raised hay and his wife set up her camp stove again. This time she called her restaurant Wilson's Hotel. Guests used stumps for tables and slept in haystacks. "Housekeeping was not difficult then," Luzena remembered, with no "windows to wash or carpets to take up."

*Some women in the mines dressed in men's clothing for ease and comfort.*

For a while, the Wilsons' hotel was the only structure on the road from Sacramento to Benicia. As neighbors clustered around, a small village grew up. Its residents named it Vacaville. Luzena Wilson had founded a town.

Women in California had more freedom than their sisters in the East. Nancy Gooch, still a slave when she arrived in the diggings, was freed when California became a state in 1850. She worked as a washerwoman in Coloma, earning enough money to buy her son's freedom in Missouri. (He later bought Sutter's sawmill.)

*Langton and Brothers Express Office, where miners could exchange gold dust for cash or buy a stagecoach ticket out of town*

Women in the diggings worked as hard as the men and sometimes took on jobs that were not usually thought of as "women's work." Women operated bowling alleys and saloons and sold real estate. They became detectives for the Wells Fargo stage company, helping to catch bandits. One woman, who called herself Charley Pankhurst, worked as a stage driver for years, disguised as a man. Friends discovered her true identity only after she died.

California had incorporated Mexican law into its constitution, giving women the right to own property and to buy and sell land—rights they didn't have in the eastern states. If a woman in California married a man who treated her badly, it was easier to get a divorce. Emigrant women missed their friends and relatives back home but not the strict rules about the way they should behave. "I am a worshipper at the shrine of liberty," Jennie Megquier announced.

Dame Shirley, who had led a sheltered, well-to-do life in the East, also preferred the rough life of California. "Really," she told her sister, "everybody ought to go the mines, just to see how little it takes to make people comfortable in the world."

# Children in the Mines

A mother uses a miner's cradle to rock her baby.

Like other young people who struggled over the Sierras with their parents in the cold days of October, fourteen-year-old Sallie Hester was "worn out" as well as a little skeptical about Vernon, the small town near Sacramento where her parents had chosen to live. "This is a funny looking town anyway. Most of the houses are built of brush," Sallie wrote in her diary. The fall rains began, and the Hesters hurried to find shelter. Sallie's father paid a carpenter to build them a two-room house, whose one luxury was a rough floor made of hand-hewn logs. After five months of sleeping in tents and wagons, Sallie was pleased to have a home, but their first Christmas was dreary. Sallie's mother was homesick, and Sallie was depressed by the rain, which flooded the Sacramento and Feather Rivers near their cabin.

"Nearly everybody is up to their knees in mud and water," Sallie wrote. "Some have boots. As far as the eye can reach you see nothing but water. It's horrible. Wish I was back in Indiana. Snakes are plenty. They come down the river, crawl under our beds and everywhere."

*Our party of fifty wagons, now only thirteen, has at last reached this haven of rest. Strangers in a strange land — what will the future be?* — Sallie Hester

But Sallie didn't stay sad long. Soon after she arrived, she was surrounded by young men. She had thought she was "too young for beaux, but the men don't seem to think so." Men outnumbered women in the diggings twenty to one. At dances, girls as young as four were pulled onto the dance floor.

Many girls married by the time they were teenagers. One family arrived in California with two daughters, ages fifteen and seventeen. As they were setting up their tent the first night, small groups of men arrived to flirt and look them over. Three days later, the younger daughter ran away to get married, and a week later, her older sister was engaged.

Men in the camps were homesick for the families they'd left behind, so they treasured the few children who arrived in the diggings. Miners told

*A crowd of miners proudly surround the only two children in their camp.*

*Young Indian boys sometimes found jobs working for the miners.*

them stories, taught them to read, and brought them small gifts. If a photographer came to town to take pictures, the miners placed the children in the front of the picture, as if they were royalty. The birth of a baby was a special event. Work stopped, and the miners welcomed the new child by firing guns into the air, cooking special food, and making up songs.

In spite of the hardships of the first few years, many children enjoyed life in the diggings. They had more freedom than they were used to in the eastern states. Girls, especially, led very different lives. In the East, young girls were often confined to the house, where they worked alongside their mothers. But in the small mining camps, girls spent most of the day outside, hauling water from the river, caring for younger siblings, tending animals, or gathering firewood.

Boys could earn money at a young age. They became camp cooks for organized companies of miners or helped to operate rockers or Long Toms, earning a share of the gold. They hunted for quail, rabbits, and other small game to share with their families or to sell to hungry prospectors.

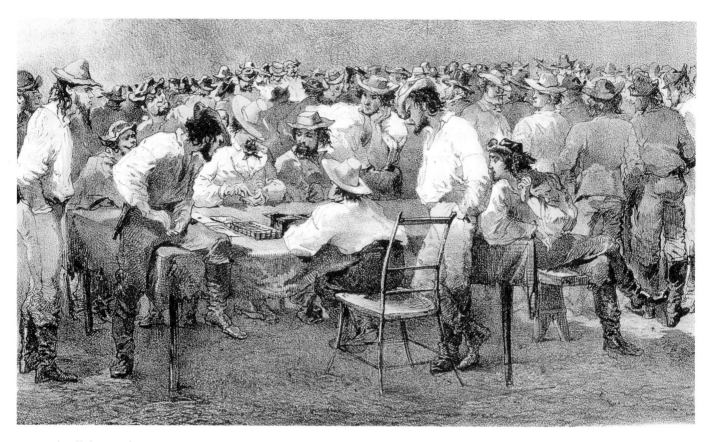

As they roamed about the camps, boys and girls saw the seedy side of the diggings. Gambling was the most popular form of entertainment, and children learned early how to play cards and bet. Many parents were upset by the swearing and rough language their children heard and by their exposure to prostitution, stealing, and violence, which was common in the more crowded camps. In one twenty-four-hour period, Dame Shirley reported, her mining camp had "twenty-four murders, fearful accidents, bloody deaths, a mob, whippings, a hanging, an attempt at suicide, and a fatal duel." Many parents worried, just as they do today, that their children would become more violent if they watched other people behave violently.

Life was uncertain for children. Like the grown-ups, they suffered from scurvy the first few winters, and some died of cholera, diphtheria, or dysentery. Because it was easier for men and women to get divorced in California, some children grew up being raised by one parent. Others were orphaned when their parents died of diseases or in accidents. The lucky ones were adopted by lonely miners, but some had to shift for themselves.

Children helped their parents survive. If a family ran a store, laundry, or boardinghouse, children scrubbed clothes, washed dishes, set tables, and chopped wood for the fire. Fresh fruits and vegetables were scarce, so children went foraging in the forest for purslane, wild onions, berries, and other plants. Some learned about local edible plants from Native American children. They would bring the plants back to their parents or sell them to other miners.

*I was the luckiest one in the group, and found a nugget worth five dollars.*

— Martha Gentry

Children also caught gold fever. Martha Gentry was eleven when she started mining in Placerville. "One day a miner gave me and the other children permission to dig on his claim," she wrote. "Diligently we set out to work, and carefully scooped up the soft dirt and then washed it, just as we had seen the men do many times. I was the luckiest one in the group, and found a nugget worth five dollars. With this I bought a new pair of

*A mining couple with their child*

*Children enjoyed watching miners at work. Some, like Martha Gentry, collected gold dust.*

shoes of which I was sorely in need, for the moccasins given me by the old Indian squaw were now worn out."

When one of the miners bet that she couldn't predict the weight of a small nugget, Martha surprised him by guessing accurately. Soon she was winning many small gold pieces this way. "In a short time," Martha said, "I became so expert that I had accumulated a...hoard of gold, and was in fair way to make my fortune."

Children also "prospected" for gold in stores and saloons. Miners paid for everything with gold dust, which spilled easily. Children came in after closing and ran wet pins between the cracks in the floorboards to pick up the dust.

Many camp children became bold and independent. They ignored their parents' warnings about Native Americans and cautiously visited their settlements, getting to know native children and learning a few words of their language.

There were few schools in the mining towns, and books were scarce, so children made their own entertainment. They played games: Anti-I-Over, Pop the Whip, and Wolf Over the River. They learned to play musical instruments and to dance, sometimes by sneaking into dance halls and saloons to watch the performers who traveled from town to town. A few discovered they had talent and became entertainers themselves. Boys and girls from Germany and Czechoslovakia dressed in native costume and performed dances they had learned in Europe, while other children accompanied them on the tambourine, organ, or violin.

*Children spent most of their time outdoors, often doing chores. Here, two boys gather cow chips.*

Most children who worked made small amounts of money, enough to help their parents buy food or to allow them to afford some extras such as shoes. But one little girl in the gold rush made more money when she was eight years old than her father, who first worked as a miner and then ran a hotel.

Her name was Lotta Crabtree.

From the moment she arrived in San Francisco in 1853, Lotta's bright red hair, black eyes, and lively personality made heads turn. Like her mother, Mary, Lotta could imitate anyone. She was quick to learn dances and songs and could recite poems and stories. The Crabtrees settled in the town of Rabbit Creek, and Mary enrolled Lotta in dancing school. Lotta and her mother also made friends with Lola Montez, a Spanish performer known all over the world for her famous—and slightly shocking—"Spider Dance." Montez taught Lotta more jigs, reels, and songs.

Lola Montez

When Lotta was eight, her mother took her into a local saloon to perform. The audience terrified her. "The hall was full of miners," Lotta remembered. "There were candles for footlights, and the room smelled strongly of tobacco smoke. I stepped bravely out." Once she was standing in front of the audience, Lotta was transformed. Her black eyes sparkled; her body was taut and full of energy. She could laugh and sing at the same time.

Lotta's mother found a violinist to accompany her daughter, and they went on a tour of the diggings. They played in hotels, saloons, and gambling halls, in little camps such as Port Wine, Quincy, and Bidwell's Bar, where patrons made a stage by pushing two pool tables together. Every night, Lotta had stage fright. And every night, Mary Crabtree forced her onstage, then watched as Lotta forgot her fear and charmed the audience.

*When I was through they roared with applause so much that I was terrified and they threw to me nuggets of gold. That started my stage career.*

— *Lotta Crabtree*

After each performance, Mary Crabtree strapped Lotta to the saddle of a mule. Lotta fell asleep as the mule picked its way down the steep trails leading into the next town. Before long, Lotta was playing small parts in San Francisco theaters. By the time she was a teenager, she was a rich and popular comedian, entertaining audiences as far away as New York and London.

Of course, Lotta's story was unusual. Most children didn't make their fortune in the mines. But many became more independent, more adaptable, and eager for adventure than they might have if they'd stayed in the eastern states. This was especially true for children who grew up in the town nicknamed Phoenix City, after the mythical bird that rises from the ashes.

*Lotta Crabtree*

# Phoenix City

*Yuerba Buena (now San Francisco) in 1837*

Two years before the gold rush began, San Francisco was a sleepy village called Yerba Buena, after the Spanish term for the wild mint growing on its many hills. Coyotes, wildcats, rabbits, and quail lived in the brush surrounding the village, which was home to about eight hundred people, including sixty children. The town boasted two gristmills—one powered by sails, the other by mules—and a small hotel called the Leidesdorff, named for a successful West Indian businessman. The hotel had a billiards room, a small restaurant, and a bar where Californios played a card game called monte.

Yerba Buena grew up around a deep, protected port, ideal for ships of all sizes. If a boat appeared in the town's glistening harbor, it caused a sensation. A young resident remembered climbing eagerly "through the thickets and wild shrubs—almost impenetrable for a child—up over two or three hills...to see the first ocean steamer come in.... The hill was crowded black with people."

One early arrival was a three-masted clipper named the *Brooklyn*, which brought Sam Brannan and a group of Mormon pioneers to town in 1846. Seventeen-year-old Edward Kemble was also on board. A young printer from Troy, New York, Kemble had brought a printing press, a set of movable type, and a block of wood with the name of the town's future newspaper—the *California Star*—cut into it.

Within a few months, Kemble and Brannan set up the press on the second floor of a gristmill and began printing the *Star*. "While the type was being set in the loft for the first sheet," Kemble remembered, "a mule was grinding out grain on the ground floor below, on which a part of the townspeople were fed."

By the time the English artist J.D. Borthwick disembarked there in 1851, the town was no longer the sleepy backwater that had greeted

*A tangle of masts filled San Francisco's harbor in the early days of the gold rush.*

*You must bless your stars you are not here at present.... Six thousand people...have no shelter.... The wind blows enough to take your head off, so we set here all huddled together.*

—Jennie Megquier

young Kemble. It had become San Francisco, the first full-fledged city in the West. "Everything bore evidence of newness," Borthwick wrote.

The city's streets were not paved with gold, as the emigrants had expected. In fact, they weren't paved at all. Struggling up the hills along streets that were dusty in the dry season, thick with mud in the winter, new visitors heard a chorus of different languages. They bought melons from Chinese vendors carrying fruit in deep baskets and held out their boots to Frenchmen or African Americans

*San Francisco's Chinatown*

for blackening. They listened as young newsboys called out headlines in French, German, Swedish, Chinese, Italian, and Spanish. They heard about upcoming plays and entertainment from African-American bell ringers who walked from one neighborhood to the next, working to draw crowds into the theaters.

Borthwick explored the town and found that "the streets presented a scene of intense bustle and excitement." He passed crowds of bearded miners pushing into gambling houses or theaters. He walked through vibrant Chinatown, where red ribbons streamed from the doorways and

*In eight short years, San Francisco became a bustling port. Sacramento Street boasted a library that included books written in French and Spanish.*

signs in Chinese characters advertised fans and shawls; tea, dried fish, and ducks; or copper pots and kettles. He drew back when someone announced, "A muss!" or fight, and "a mob collected on the street in a moment." And he dodged the rats, which grew to "an enormous size." (One enterprising merchant imported a shipload of cats to deal with the rat problem.)

Borthwick was one of hundreds of new arrivals who poured into the city every day. Like the men in the diggings, they needed housing, clean clothes, and fresh food. Some searched for a doctor; others wanted to buy mining tools. Many men and women, such as Mifflin Gibbs, decided to stay in San Francisco and provide the emigrants with the services they needed.

Gibbs had no job and no way to pay the twelve dollars he owed his landlord for a bed. Following his motto, "Never disclose your poverty until the last gleam of hope has sunk," he went to the nearest construction site and talked the boss into giving him a job, then bought tools from a nearby store on credit.

By the end of the week, Gibbs had repaid his debts, but he was out of work again. The white workers at the construction site had threatened to quit if their boss kept a black man on the job. So Gibbs became a bootblack. It was considered menial work, but it paid well, since men and women needed to protect their shoes against the city's ankle-deep

*California was often said to be famous for three things: rats, fleas, and empty bottles.* —J.D. Borthwick

mud. Before long, Gibbs had earned enough money to go into partnership with Peter Lester, a skilled African-American boot maker. Many San Franciscans bought their footwear at Lester and Gibbs's "Emporium for Fine Boots and Shoes, Imported from Philadelphia, London, and Paris."

New arrivals also needed to get their clothes washed. For a long time, San Francisco had no running water, and some residents sent their shirts as far away as the Sandwich Islands, Hawaii, or even China, paying up to twelve dollars a dozen for clean shirts. Others simply wore their shirts and pants until they fell apart, then bought new ones. Native American and

*Looking down on*
*Washerwomen's Bay in 1856*

Mexican women realized they could offer a cheaper alternative and began washing clothes at a pond soon known as Washerwomen's Bay.

Washerwomen's Bay became a popular spot. In 1851, the newspaper *Alta California* reported that there were usually two to three hundred people there, with "pillowcases, shirts, sheets, and unmentionables" flying in the air like flags. When people complained about high prices, up to eight dollars to wash a dozen articles of clothing, the women formed a society to protect their wages. By 1853, Chinese laundrymen had also moved into Washerwomen's Bay, adding an ironing service.

Thousands of San Francisco's children found jobs as the city's population exploded. Boys and girls worked in stores, sharpened knives, helped surveyors lay out new streets, dug ditches, and helped out in restaurants, hotels, and laundries. Only a few went to school.

By 1855, San Francisco published more different newspapers than the city of London, and selling newspapers was the prize job for young boys. J.D. Borthwick heard their "shrill voices" all over town, "crying their various papers." A newsboy's pay was good, and newspapers from the eastern United States were especially valuable, even though the news might be six or eight months old.

Newsboys stood on San Francisco's steep hills overlooking the harbor, signaling to one another as ships entered the bay. The moment a ship was in sight, they raced to the wharf, grabbed a bundle of papers, then hurried to the steamship docks, where boats loaded cargo for the trip up the Sacramento River. Sly boys stowed away on the steamers to avoid paying the fare, then reappeared when the ship was underway to sell their papers to passengers. A newsboy caught without a ticket had to shovel coal into the ship's boiler. Once the boats reached Sacramento or Stockton, newsboys sold the rest of their papers to storekeepers or peddlers headed for the mining camps. Newsboys were proud of their status and appearance and

*Newspaper Row, where many of San Francisco's newspapers were published, including the* EVENING PICAYUNE *and Sam Brannan's* HERALD.

*A San Francisco sheriff and*
*his daughter*

often wore fancy clothes as they roamed the city streets crying out the latest headlines. Many boys weren't content to just sell papers and started newspapers of their own.

Most city children lived in hotels or rooming houses with no backyards, so the city's dusty streets became their playgrounds. They played marbles on the wooden sidewalks, using holes in the boards as part of the obstacles in the game. They flew kites in the stiff wind, raced homemade carts down the city's steep hills, and begged sweets from a street seller called the Lump Man, because his pockets bulged with candy. The city was known for its exotic pet population, and children loved to watch people pass with their parrots, raccoons, bears, and burros.

Children came to San Francisco from every corner of the world. They learned bits of each other's languages as they played games together or shared meals in rooming houses. As in the mining camps, the city's children had a loose, unstructured life. They might live in a tent one week, a rooming house the next. Children shifted for themselves as their parents struggled to buy an expensive building lot or to pay high rent for a few cramped rooms.

San Francisco also had a large number of orphans, as many as 270 by 1851, whose parents had died from disease or in accidents on the way to California. If they weren't among the lucky few taken in by other families, they lived in shanties and organized themselves into street gangs, playing pranks on Chinese immigrants and stealing from any shopkeeper whose back was turned.

*We have again been obliged to pack up our duds, expecting every minute to be burnt out.*

— *Jennie Megquier*

As fast as the new city grew, it burned down. On Christmas Eve in 1849, an African-American man ordered a drink in a bar. The bar-

*Fires frequently raged through San Francisco.*

*A San Francisco fire brigade*

tender told him it was a white man's bar and ordered him to leave. A fight broke out, a kerosene lamp fell over, and two city blocks burned to the ground. They were rebuilt, but a fire raged again in May. A month later, four hundred buildings burned. And in the spring of 1851, more than two thousand buildings went up in flames. But San Franciscans didn't stay down for long. Residents put up new buildings while the fires were still smoldering.

Crime increased with the booming population. Mifflin Gibbs was sitting in his boot shop on a Sunday morning, when the "plank street resounded with the tramp of a multitude." He ran to the door and watched five thousand men march by, carrying rifles over their shoulders. They belonged to Sam Brannan's Vigilance Committee, a group of angry citizens who were disgusted by San Francisco's lack of police force and by its corrupt city government. They took over the city for three months,

*The Vigilance Committee showed its strength by parading through San Francisco's streets.*

making their own rules, arresting people, and punishing them without trials.

Mifflin Gibbs soon learned that California had two rules of law: one for whites and another for everyone else. When a white customer stormed into his shop and beat Gibbs's partner, Peter Lester, with a cane, Lester didn't resist. Both men knew it would be useless to report the assault, because a person of color was not allowed to testify against a white man in court.

In the end, Gibbs decided to leave San Francisco. He spoke out against racism in California as boldly as he had in Philadelphia, and when the state threatened to exclude free blacks from entering the state, Gibbs joined the rush to the Fraser River goldfields, in British Columbia.

Another group of newcomers would also face a cold welcome in the growing city. These were the people Californians called the Celestials, men from China who began arriving by the boatload in 1852, in search of a land they called Gold Mountain.

# Gold Mountain

*Unidentified Chinese man,*
*San Francisco, 1850*

The Chinese left few written records of their life in California, so we don't know for certain how news of the gold rush traveled across the Pacific. It may have been spread by a Cantonese miner named Chum Ming, who struck it rich at Sutter's mill and wrote home to tell his relatives about his good fortune.

In 1848, census figures listed only three nameless Chinese as California residents. Two years after Chum Ming's success, more than four hundred Chinese had made the long journey to the land the Cantonese called Gum San, or Gold Mountain. By 1852, about twenty thousand Chinese men were living in the state, including two thousand who had arrived in San Francisco in a single day.

Most Chinese immigrants were young men fleeing terrible poverty. They did not intend to stay in California, and most had promised their families they would return as soon as they had made their fortune.

One young dreamer was a sixteen-year-old named Lee Chew. Chew grew up in the province of Canton, China, in a house made of blue brick. Although famines and wars had torn his country apart, the Lee family lived comfortably on their small farm. By the time he was ten, Lee Chew was working in his father's fields. Each day, he visited his grandfather, who told him stories about the terrible red-haired *fan qui*, or foreign devils, in America.

When Lee Chew turned sixteen, a neighbor who had emigrated to America as a poor young man suddenly returned home with full pockets. He took "ground as large as four city blocks and made a paradise of it." The neighbor invited the whole town to a banquet at his new palace, where he served a hundred roasted pigs and "such an abundance of dainties that our villagers even now lick their fingers when they think of it."

Lee Chew made up his mind. In spite of his grandfather's warnings, he would take a ship to Gum San. At first, his parents protested, but finally Chew's father gave his son his blessing and sent him off with one hundred dollars—a small fortune in those days—which paid for his passage on a steamer and left him fifty dollars to spend when he reached San Francisco.

Most Chinese crossed the Pacific in small boats, crammed below deck in dark cabins smelling of sweat and vomit, their bunks piled up "like stacks of coffins in a death house." The food was so bad and the seas so rough that one immigrant carved these words on the wall of Angel Island when he arrived: "I ate wind and tasted waves for more than twenty days." Others, like Lee Chew, were "afraid to eat the provisions of the barbarians." Epidemics swept through the holds of the ships. Some men, who had been tricked into emigrating, were chained to the boats and beaten when they tried to escape. A few threw themselves into the sea in despair.

*I ate wind and tasted waves for more than twenty days.*
— *Carved on a wall at Angel Island*

Those who survived staggered off the ships four to eight weeks later, carrying their few belongings in double-ended baskets slung across their shoulders, their long black queues, or single braids, hanging to their waists, their faces hidden under broad-brimmed hats.

Americans and Europeans were fascinated by the men they called the Celestials. They welcomed the early Chinese ships, eager to trade gold dust for precious goods on board: dried fruit, candied ginger, lumber, brocaded silks—even houses, shipped in pieces.

Some Chinese found "Gold Mountain" right in San Francisco and never went to the mines. They took jobs in small restaurants with the Chinese characters ENTER AND DEPART IN PEACE written on flags over

*A Chinese restaurant
in San Francisco*

the doors. They sold vegetables or worked in gambling dens. Many, like Lee Chew, opened laundries.

In China, washing clothes was considered women's work, but a man in America could start a laundry without too much money, even if he didn't speak English. Young Lee Chew's first job was working for an American woman and her family. She taught him how to wash and iron the family's clothes, sent him to school to learn English, and paid him $3.50 a week. Even though Lee Chew sent money home to his parents, he saved most of his earnings. In two years, he was able to open his own hand laundry.

Most Chinese arrivals, though, headed straight for the diggings, where they were an instant curiosity. Many Americans and Europeans had never encountered Asian people. The artist J.D. Borthwick was particularly interested in the Chinese he met in the mines. Coming on one group at supper time, he sketched the men as they cooked dinner and braided each other's queues. "They squatted on the rocks in groups of eight or ten round a number of curious little black pots and dishes, from which they helped themselves with their chopsticks," Borthwick wrote. The Chinese

*The Chinese established laundries in mining camps as well as in larger towns.*

*This sketch by J.D. Borthwick shows Chinese miners relaxing after a day in the diggings.*

welcomed him warmly, offering to share their meal, but he was too nervous about their unusual food to accept.

Chinese miners were usually organized into companies of fifty or more men. They used a device known as a Chinese waterwheel, a series of buckets operated by pulleys. They diverted the water in the streams with wing dams, which cut the stream in half, leaving the rocky bottom exposed and dry for digging. Working long hours, seven days a week, they often extracted gold from places where less determined prospectors had given up. Their first prosperous claim, on Wood's Creek, became known as the Chinese Diggings.

Many Chinese miners took their shares of gold to jewelers, where it was made into ornaments and belts. These could be stitched into clothing and hidden from American customs agents, so they wouldn't have to pay a duty on their earnings when they returned to China.

Before long, Chinese success in the diggings made other miners angry. Whenever they heard about a new Chinese strike, jealous American and European miners drove the Chinese out. They stoned them, burned their houses, broke up their equipment, hacked off their queues, and sometimes

*Some Americans learned valuable mining skills from Chinese miners.*

murdered them, knowing they wouldn't be punished. "White men are not usually hanged for killing Chinamen," the *San Francisco Bulletin* stated casually.

Violence against the Chinese also broke out in San Francisco. Children stoned Chinese workers, broke their bamboo baskets, and taunted them while their parents looked the other way. Restaurant owners fired their Chinese cooks or kept their identity a secret. People made fun of the Chinese for their loose clothing, their wooden shoes, and their habit of drinking tea. (If Americans had boiled their water as the Chinese did, they could have avoided dysentery.) Even some

*The manners and habits of the Chinese are very repugnant to Americans in California. Of different language, blood, religion, and character, and inferior in most mental and bodily qualities, the Chinaman is looked upon by some as only a little superior to the Negro, and by others as somewhat inferior.*

—THE ANNALS OF SAN FRANCISCO

*A propaganda poster from the Workingmen's Party, urging the removal of the Chinese from California*

Native Americans, who were treated as badly as the Chinese, looked down on the arrivals from Asia. When someone was told he "didn't have a Chinaman's chance," it meant his situation was hopeless.

Lee Chew's experience was similar to that of many other immigrants to Gum San. His laundry customers cheated him and stole bundles of clothing. When he became a merchant, he decided that Americans "treat you as a friend while you are prosperous, but if you have a misfortune, they don't know you." Every day, he put up with insults.

*How can I call this my home, and how can anyone blame me if I take my money and go back to my village in China?*
*— Lee Chew*

Even though he realized that not all Americans were "foreign devils," he insisted, until the end of his life, that "their treatment of us is outrageous."

Unfortunately the Chinese were not the only people being hounded by Americans. By the early 1850s, an undeclared, ugly war against most foreigners was breaking out all over California.

# Blood Scattered Like Water

*A few short years of mining altered life along the riverbanks forever.*

On October 18, 1850, the steamer *Oregon* churned into San Francisco's harbor, bringing news from Washington, D.C.: California had been admitted to the Union! The city held an instant celebration. Citizens lit bonfires, set off cannons, and gathered in cheering mobs in Portsmouth Square. Newspapers from the East, reporting the vote in Congress, sold for five dollars a copy.

The reaction was different in the hills, where miners were battling the fall rains. As they struggled to save their cabins, flumes, and Long Toms from the flooding, the issue of California's statehood seemed distant and unimportant. Besides, they had a more serious worry: The surface gold was disappearing fast. Instead of wading into a stream with a shovel and a gold pan, prospectors now had to dig deep into the hillsides for gold embedded in the rock and then use more complicated techniques to extract the precious metal. Often this required heavy, expensive machinery to crush the rock as well as a large labor force.

For the first time since gold was discovered, traffic began to flow in two directions. Thousands of discouraged miners poured into San Francisco, hoping to book passage home, while newcomers, just off the boats, headed for the diggings, puzzled by the downcast expressions of men ashamed to admit they had given up.

The Americans who stayed still hoped for a bonanza. They took a sharp look at the thousands of strangers competing with them for smaller and smaller takings. Who were these people who spoke unusual languages, looked different, and followed strange customs and religions? If California was a state, American miners wondered, shouldn't its gold belong to them and not to these "foreigners"?

*Miners enjoyed posing for group pictures, as in this daguerreotype taken around 1850.*

American miners began to make their own rules about who belonged in the diggings. In the southern mines, near the Merced and Stanislaus Rivers, they turned their fury on Spanish-speaking people, lumping them all together as "greasers," whether they had been born in Mexico, Chile, or California.

Violence against Latinos became widespread. In the town of Downieville, a Mexican woman known only as Josefa was lynched by an angry mob. According to rumors, she had stabbed a white man who broke into her home. A local newspaper reported that "she was immediately arrested, tried, sentenced and hung at four o'clock in the afternoon of the same day. She did not exhibit the least fear, walking up a small ladder to the scaffold, and placing the rope round her neck with her own hands, first gracefully removing two plaits of raven black hair from her shoulders."

*Had this woman been an American instead of a Mexican, instead of being hung for the deed, she would have been lauded for it. It was not her guilt which condemned this unfortunate woman, but her Mexican blood.*
— *Newspaper account*

Nearly a thousand people watched her die. In a similar case, Dame Shirley wrote to her sister about a Spaniard in Rich Bar who dared ask an American to repay a loan. "The poor Spaniard received, for an answer, several inches of cold steel in his breast, which inflicted a very dangerous wound. Nothing was done, and very little was said about this atrocious affair."

American prospectors who had arrived as ignorant greenhorns forgot that many Sonorans as well as local Californios had graciously taught them how to pan for gold. The terms *bonanza* and *placer mining*, both taken from the Spanish, had become part of every miner's working vocabulary. But suddenly Americans resented the successes of Mexicans and Californios.

Some emigrants decided to give up mining altogether and become farmers. They squatted on *ranchos*, claiming the land as their own. Why should the Californios own such big tracts of land? the Americans demanded. Why not carve the *ranchos* up into smaller plots, the way farms were divided back in New England? They didn't understand that vast amounts of pasture land were required to support a herd of cattle in California's dry climate. And they had forgotten that California's constitution granted legal and property rights to local Californios. Determined to drive the Californios out, squatters burned their crops, shot stray cattle, tore down any unoccupied buildings, and blocked the gates to their *ranchos*.

Mariano Guadalupe Vallejo, one of the wealthiest Californios in the state, had once owned more than two hundred thousand acres of land. Vallejo, his wife, Benicia, and their sixteen children were known for their gracious hospitality. During the Mexican-American War, Vallejo woke in the middle of the night to shouts and pounding on his door. American soldiers had come to arrest him. Always the perfect host, Vallejo offered them a bottle of wine while he went to get dressed.

Now his kindness to American invaders was forgotten. Squatters seized his lands, burned his crops, and drove off his Indian laborers. Vallejo fought the seizures, lost many court battles, and finally gave up. He sold his meager holdings and moved to San Francisco. "The Master of the land wishes his own well-being, and not ours!" he protested bitterly.

*Mariano Guadalupe Vallejo, (above) and his rancho, Lachryma Montis (below)*

*These legal thieves, clothed in the robes of the law, took from us our lands and our houses, and without the least scruple enthroned themselves in our homes like so many powerful kings.*

— *Mariano Guadalupe Vallejo*

In Sacramento in 1850, the California legislature passed a Foreign Miners' Tax of twenty dollars a month. Although many miners were foreign-born, having emigrated from European countries, the law was printed in English and Spanish, and the state took the money mainly from Spanish-speaking people. Thousands of Mexicans and Chileans, forced to give up their claims, returned home.

The influx of gold seekers was even more destructive for California's native population than it was for the Californios. Ever since the first gold nugget was discovered on Nisenan Indian land, at Sutter's sawmill, Indians throughout the region had been struggling to find ways to cope with the invasion.

*Whites, Native Americans, and Californios worked together only as long as gold was plentiful.*

When the gold rush began, some native people, who were already used to a nomadic life, fled to more remote mountain areas. Some tried to defend their lands by attacking the invaders. Many prospected for gold themselves. When Governor Mason toured the area near Sutter's mill in the summer of 1848, he reported seeing thousands of Native Americans panning with willow baskets.

Other Native Americans realized that they had an advantage over the arriving miners. After all, they outnumbered the prospectors ten to one, and they often knew where to find gold. Those who were willing to share their skills hired themselves out to Californios or to early arrivals from Mexico and Oregon. They took their pay in traded goods, but miners and merchants often cheated them, using a lead slug known as a Digger's ounce to weigh their gold dust. A Digger's ounce actually weighed two ounces, which meant that Native Americans had to use twice as much gold to pay for their goods as other miners did.

As more miners poured onto their lands, a few Native Americans acted as agents between their own people and the miners, providing the prospectors with cheap, skilled labor. One man who was very successful in this business was the Miwok José Jesús. At the time gold was discovered, Jesús was chief of a small Native American village called a *ranchería*. When miners advanced into diggings along the Stanislaus River, Jesús recruited Yokut and Miwok laborers for a man named Charles Weber. Under Jesús's direction, Northern Yokuts discovered

*If ever an Indian was fully and honestly paid for his labor, it was not my luck to hear of it.*

— *Anonymous settler*

*Many native families became homeless when their lands were seized by miners.*

*Some Indians took shelter in Yosemite's wilderness.*

one of the richest gold deposits in the state, on Carson's Creek, helping James Carson pan out 180 ounces of gold in ten days. Jesús paid his workers in meat, beans, sugar, and coffee.

Miwoks working with Jesús used entire families to pan for gold. The men dug up the mud and gravel, then passed it to their children, who carried it to women working in groups along the streambed. Women washed out the gold in their tightly woven grass baskets, then tied it up in rags.

Most native people were not as lucky as the Miwoks and Yokuts who worked for José Jesús. Before the arrival of the miners, Native Americans had lived well on California's wide variety of wild plants and animals. But mining soon destroyed much of the natural landscape that had fed and nourished them. The constant activity in and around the rivers drove away the game, killed the fish, polluted the water, and weakened the oak trees, shrinking their

*The poverty and misery that now exists among these Indians is beyond description.*

— E. A. Stevenson, special Indian agent

once-bountiful acorn harvests. E. A. Stevenson, a government agent who visited many Indian settlements at the end of the gold rush, wrote to Washington: "The poverty and misery that now exists among these Indians is beyond description.... The miners have turned the streams from their beds and conveyed the water to the dry diggings, and after...it is so thick with mud that it will scarcely run; it returns to its natural channel, and with it the soil from a thousand hills, which has driven almost every kind of fish to seek new resort."

By the early 1850s, there were twice as many whites as Native Americans in California, and most agreed with the editor of the *San Francisco Bulletin*, who wrote, "It is a painful necessity of advancing civilization that the Indians should gradually disappear."

Violence against Native Americans erupted throughout the diggings. Some camps offered rewards for native scalps or for Indian heads brought in on stakes. Other miners proudly called themselves Squaw Hunters.

*A posed picture of Paiutes and white surveyors taken during construction of a road from Mojave, Arizona, to San Bernadino, California*

One of the worst incidents was the Bloody Island Massacre of 1850, in which a huge party of white soldiers slaughtered hundreds of Pomo men, women, and children, stabbing babies in front of their mothers and throwing their bodies in the water. One young Pomo, captured by soldiers, was forced to march barefoot over sharp rocks until his feet were bloody. When he could hardly stand, the soldiers rubbed salt into his wounds and then laughed while he screamed in pain. As he later told Pomo chief William Benson, he wept all day, thinking, "Here I am not to see my mother and sister but to see their blood scattered over the ground like water and their bodies for coyotes to devour."

*We hope that the Government will render such aid as will enable the citizens of the north to carry on a war of extermination until the last Redskin of these tribes has been killed.* — YREKA HERALD, 1853

In 1850, the California legislature passed an Act for the Protection of Indians, which didn't protect Native Americans at all. Instead, it permitted people to kidnap Native American children and sell them for fifty dollars to anyone who needed a servant. The passage of this law broke up thousands of Native American families, including that of the young Wailiki Lucy Young.

Lucy Young

When Lucy was twelve, she was captured by white soldiers. She and her mother and sister escaped and spent the next few weeks on the run, traveling at night, sleeping by day, living on grasshoppers, roots, berries, and two ducks, which Lucy scooped up in the skirt the soldiers had forced her to wear. As they climbed Lassik's Peak, they grew weak from thirst. "I starve for water," Lucy remembered. "I hunt for water like in redwoods, see li'l ferns, drink water, carry to mother.... Too hungry we feel."

Finally they holed up in a "lonesome" valley, where they built a bark house, hoping to spend the winter. But soldiers from Seward's Fort caught them. Lucy was separated from her mother and sent to live with a white man who beat his wife. Afraid he would mistreat her, too, Lucy let her captor's horses out of the barn and ran away. Carrying nothing but a small box of matches, Lucy walked barefoot through deep snow to find her mother, who had also been kidnapped by a white man. She brought her mother some food, then left for a Wailiki settlement called Poison Rock to look for her sister.

"Young girl lay there, sick, my half sister. That night she die. Snowing, raining hard. They dig hole right by house, put body in. All went out. Tore all house down, set it afire. Midnight, snow whirl, wind howl."

Lucy's horrors weren't over. She was caught again, this time by a man who treated her as his wife, although she was still a young girl. She had many children with him; only one survived. Her father and brother were killed by soldiers. When she was an old woman, Lucy told her story so that her people would not be forgotten. "White people want our land, want destroy us," she said. "I hear people tell 'bout what Inyan do early days to white man. Nobody ever tell it what white man do to Inyan. That's reason I tell it. That's history. That's truth. I seen it myself."

*I hear people tell 'bout what Inyan do early days to white man. Nobody ever tell it what white man do to Inyan.*

— Lucy Young

Lucy's story was not unique. Before the first gold nugget was found at Sutter's mill, as many as 150,000 Native Americans lived throughout the state of California. By 1860, less than thirty thousand remained. The prophecy of Lucy's Wailiki grandfather—that his people would have "no more, this world"—had come to pass.

# The End of La Fiebre del Oro

As gold disappeared in California, miners moved on to other strikes, such as Pikes Peak.

**B**y 1858, only ten years after gold was discovered at Sutter's mill, the rush was over. Only those who had enough capital to buy big machinery could now hope to earn money in the diggings. Prospectors who were still infected with gold fever moved on to new El Dorados: Nevada's Comstock Lode, the Fraser River in British Columbia, Pikes Peak in Colorado.

The gold rush was a coin with both a bright and a dark side. It offered many people, from all over the world, a chance for fresh beginnings. African Americans who had been slaves bought their freedom. Women who had never earned money supported their families. Children became independent and adventurous. Young men who had arrived penniless created wildly successful businesses. And a few lucky miners really did pluck a fortune from rivers and streams overnight.

*A group of miners and their families, using water under pressure to extract gold from the hillside. Most miners couldn't afford such expensive equipment.*

Although many bustling mining camps later became ghost towns, the gold rush opened the West. Until 1846, Kansas had marked the western edge of American settlement. The overland migration and the discovery of gold and silver in new areas lured miners, ranchers, and farmers into territories that would later become the states of Arizona, New Mexico, Colorado, and Wyoming.

California's growing population pressured Congress for a transcontinental railroad to serve its booming economy. The *New York Herald* began calling for a railroad to California as soon as news of the gold strike

*Miner Charles Mitchell before leaving Massachusetts (left) and on his return home in the mid-1850s (right)*

reached the east coast. On May 10, 1869, twenty years after the first forty-niners headed west, the "golden spike" was driven, completing the railway and uniting the continent.

The dark side of the gold rush contains its sorrow: the thousands who died on the journey or in the diggings; the men and women who made fortunes only to lose them in natural disasters; the foreigners who were persecuted and driven from the mines; the Californios who watched, helpless, as their *ranchos* were chopped into tiny pieces. Children were orphaned; lonely wives waited in vain for their husbands to return; thousands crossed oceans and deserts only to realize they would have been better off if they'd stayed at home.

> *And now, my dear, allow me to ask, are your most sanguine expectations realized or at least being so? Or do you find things very much exaggerated? Would you advise anyone to go to California?*
>
> — *Sabrina Swain, to her husband, William, a miner*

Wherever gold and silver were discovered, native populations were driven from their homelands. The completion of the railroad, the slaughter

104

of the buffalo herds, and the opening of the plains to settlement would mean the end of a way of life for many western tribes.

·•·  ·•·  ·•·

Today, in the grassy valley where Ignacio Villegas once chased wild horses, Mexican Americans harvest vegetables that are shipped all over the world.

In San Francisco, a rust-gold suspension bridge spans the entrance to a bay now filled with oil tankers, sailboats, and ferries. Skyscrapers bristle on the hills where newsboys once signaled the arrival of steamships.

On Truckee Pass, an interstate cuts through the mountains, and cars drive at high speeds where Sallie Hester carried a blazing torch to guide her family over the last rocky summit.

Deep in the Sierras, at the bottom of a steep ravine, Kanaka Creek—named for the Hawaiians who mined there—meanders through a narrow valley. A tar-paper cabin stands empty under tall pines, its windows broken, a door yawning off its hinge. The creek is almost hidden behind shoulder-high piles of stones dug from the river bottoms. A dank and musty mine shaft, its ceiling crumbling, disappears into the mountainside.

Once the banks of Kanaka Creek teemed with miners. The narrow valley resounded with shouts, with the clang of hammers, the rumbling wash of stones and water in a cradle, the braying of mules stumbling down the rocky trail. Now the only sound is the creek, hissing and gurgling softly as it heads downstream, its water sparkling and clear once again.

In southern California, far from main roads, towns, or citrus groves, a dry, stony wash marks the passage of the Overland Trail from one desert valley to the next. Perched on the low rise that looks out over both valleys, Kumeyaay Indians once watched in astonishment as thousands of white men, women, and children staggered toward them under the blazing sun, their lips parched and swollen from thirst.

Now the deep ruts carved by the weight of the settlers' wagons are filled with mesquite, sage, and the tall spikes of the century plant. A place that once witnessed the transformation of the country lies still while the

desert wind whistles over the ridge, rippling the dry grass, then turns to scour the sand near empty *morteros*, the grinding rocks of Kumeyaay women.

If we listen carefully, we can imagine human sounds carried by the wind. Voices of children, pleading for water. Miners in saloons, their words a jumble of different languages. The shout of a man striking gold ("Eureka!"), mingled with a woman's desperate cries when a sudden fire consumes her cabin.

Over and under these sounds, whispering into the wind, we hear the names of California's first people. *Maidu. Yokut. Chumash. Wintu. Pomo. Nisenan. Miwok. Patwin. Kumeyaay. Luiseño. Yurok.* Their lost voices and languages still ring out, haunting the steep canyons and roaring river valleys where gold was first found.

# After the Gold Rush

**Sam Brannan** was successful as a merchant, real estate dealer, and publisher but lost six million dollars trying to start a resort in the Napa Valley. He died in an attic near San Diego, bitter and poverty-stricken.

**Juliette Brier** and her family settled in Los Angeles, where her husband preached the first Methodist sermon in southern California; then they moved north to Marysville. She had three more children, outliving all but one, and survived to age ninety-nine.

After **Lee Chew** left San Francisco, he spent three years working on the transcontinental railroad, then opened a laundry. After losing his property to vandals, he became a successful merchant in New York and returned to China for the first time in 1897.

**Louise Clappe's** letters to her sister were published in a magazine called *The Pioneer* under the pen name Dame Shirley. She and her husband moved to San Francisco and soon divorced. Clappe taught school and continued to write articles, but none were as popular as her "Letters from the California Mines." She returned to the East in her later years and died, in 1906, at age eighty-six.

**Lotta Crabtree** appeared in music halls and theaters all over California before traveling east to perform in New York. She became a popular comedian as well as an actress and singer and was also a hit in London. Her mother continued to manage Lotta's career until she retired from the stage at age forty-four. When Lotta died in Boston, her estate was worth four million dollars.

**Margaret Frink** and her husband made enough money in the hotel business to buy two dairy farms. Their foster son, Robert Parker, settled in Sacramento. At the request of friends, Ledyard Frink published his wife's diaries of their overland journey after her death.

**Mifflin Gibbs** remained active in civil rights all his life. When California threatened to keep free blacks from entering the state, Gibbs joined the rush to the Fraser River goldfields, in British Columbia. He started a store, built a railroad, and was elected to the city council. Gibbs returned to the States after the Civil War and, even though he had had no formal schooling since he was eight years old, entered Oberlin College, where he received a law degree. He practiced law in the South, was elected a city judge in Little Rock, Arkansas, and later became consul to Madagascar.

**Sallie Hester's** journal ended after she married James Maddock in a small family ceremony. "I am once more a stranger in a strange land," she wrote in her final entry. "And now, dear journal, I give thee up. No more jottings down of gay and festive scenes — the past is gone and the future is before me."

**José Jesús,** like many Native Americans of California, left no written record of his life. After 1852, his name does not appear on the census roles. He didn't sign any treaties. Did he find yet another way to adapt to the upheaval around him? Did he escape to the mountains of Yosemite? Or was he one of the tens of thousands of Native Americans who died in the gold rush? We will never know.

**Edward Kemble** left Sam Brannan's *Star* to found his own newspaper, the *Sun,* where he was known as the "boy editor." He stayed in newspaper work all his life. Years later, he enjoyed studying old sketches of San Francisco when it was known as Yerba Buena — the tiny settlement whose misty hills once overlooked an empty bay.

**Mary Jane (Jennie) Megquier** fell in love with San Francisco, where she enjoyed a freedom she had never known in Maine. Torn between her lonely children and her new life, she made three round-trips across the Isthmus of Panama. She longed for her family to join her in California, but she finally gave up hope on her third and final visit, when she traveled alone to San Francisco to settle her sick husband's business affairs. Thomas died while she was gone, and Jennie returned to Maine, full of regrets for the "frolic and dancing" and the "free and easy life" she had left behind.

The gold rush ruined **John Sutter**'s dreams of an empire, just as he had feared. He lost most of his land and cattle, his laborers abandoned him for the diggings, and vandals burned his house. He spent the last years of his life trying—unsuccessfully—to persuade Congress to repay him for his losses.

Although **Ignacio Villegas** wrote the memoir of his boyhood when he was an old man, he ended his story while he was still a vaquero, working on his father's *rancho*. He was silent about the later years that changed life completely for himself and other Californios.

**Luzena Stanley Wilson** raised three sons and a daughter while she ran her successful hotel business. In 1881, she told her daughter that "in a few more years, there will be none of us left to talk over the 'early days.'"

**Sarah Winnemucca,** or Thocmetony, became a leader of the Paiute people like her brother, father, and grandfather. Her gift for languages allowed her to act as an interpreter between her people and the U.S. military. She was also a scout for the Paiutes, once leading them to safety in the dead of night. She devoted her whole life to the Paiute tribe, traveling to eastern cities, where she described their suffering in eloquent and moving speeches. Sarah Winnemucca started the first school run by Native Americans for themselves, and her autobiography was the earliest book written in English by a Native American. She died a heroine but nearly penniless, at the home of her sister Elma in Montana.

**Lucy Young** had a number of children with the white man who forced her into marriage; she outlived all but one. In her seventies, Lucy married a Hayfork Indian named Sam. They raised horses, a cow, chickens, dogs, and cats on a small farm in Round Valley. As a little girl, her grandfather had told her, "a long time you gonta live, my child." Lucy's grandfather was right, as always. She was in her nineties when she died.

# Bibliography

## Adult Books

Baur, John E. *Growing Up with California: A History of California's Children.* Los Angeles: Will Kramer, Western American Studies Series, 1978.

Borthwick, J.D. *Three Years in California.* London: William Blackwood, 1857.

Clappe, Louise. *The Shirley Letters from the California Mines.* New York: Knopf, 1949.

Fischer, Christiane. *Let Them Speak for Themselves: Women in the American West, 1849–1900.* Hamden, Conn.: Archon, 1977.

Gibbs, Mifflin W. *Shadow and Light: An Autobiography.* New York: Arno, 1968.

Heizer, Robert F. *The Destruction of California Indians.* Santa Barbara: Peregrine Smith, 1974.

———. *The Handbook of North American Indians.* Volume 8. Washington: Smithsonian Institution, 1978.

Holliday, J. S. *The World Rushed In: The California Gold Rush Experience.* New York: Simon and Schuster, 1981.

Holmes, Kenneth L., ed. *Covered Wagon Women: Diaries and Letters from the Western Trails, 1840–1890.* Volume 2. Glendale, Calif.: Arthur H. Clark, 1983.

Holt, Hamilton, ed. *The Life Stories of Undistinguished Americans, As Told By Themselves.* New York: James Pott, 1906.

Hurtado, Albert L. *Indian Survival on the California Frontier.* New Haven: Yale University Press, 1988.

Josephy, Alvin, ed. *The American Heritage Book of the Indian.* New York: American Heritage Press, 1982.

Kemble, Edward Cleveland. *Yerba Buena—1846: Sketched Through a Loophole.* San Francisco: Johnck and Seeger, 1935.

Kingston, Maxine Hong. *China Men.* New York: Knopf, 1977.

Lapp, Rudolph M. *Blacks in Gold Rush California.* New Haven: Yale University Press, 1972.

Levy, Jo Ann. *They Saw the Elephant: Women in the California Gold Rush.* Norman, Okla.: University of Oklahoma Press, 1992.

Luchetti, Cathy. *Home on the Range: A Culinary History of the American West.* New York: Villard, 1993.

Luchetti, Cathy, and Carol Olwell. *Women of the West.* St. George, Utah: Antelope Island Press, 1982.

Megquier, Mary Jane. *Apron Full of Gold.* Albuquerque: University of New Mexico Press, 1994.

Myres, Sandra L., ed. *Ho for California! Women's Overland Diaries from the Huntington Library.* San Marino, Calif.: Henry E. Huntington Library and Art Gallery, 1980.

Nabakov, Peter, ed. *Native American Testimony: A Chronicle of Indian-White Relations from Prophecy to the Present.* New York: Viking, 1991.

Pitt, Leonard. *The Decline of the Californios.* Berkeley: University of California Press, 1966.

Rawls, James J. *Indians of California: The Changing Image.* Norman, Okla.: University of Oklahoma Press, 1984.

Rourke, Constance. *Troupers of the Gold Coast, or the Rise of Lotta Crabtree.* New York: Harcourt, Brace, 1928.

Takaki, Ronald. *A Different Mirror: A History of Multi-Cultural America.* Boston: Little, Brown, 1993.

Villegas, Ignacio. *Boyhood Days.* Edited by Dr. Albert Shumate. San Francisco: California Historical Society, 1983.

West, Elliot. *Growing Up with the Country: Childhood on the Far Western Frontier.* Albuquerque: University of New Mexico Press, 1989.

## Children's Books

Alter, Judy. *Women of the Old West.* New York: Franklin Watts, 1989.

Fisher, Leonard Everett. *The Oregon Trail.* New York: Holiday House, 1990.

Freedman, Russell. *Children of the Wild West.* New York: Clarion, 1983.

Levenson, Dorothy. *Women of the West.* New York: Franklin Watts, 1973.

McKnight, Amelia Stewart. *The Way West: Journal of a Pioneer Woman.* New York: Simon and Schuster, 1993.

Morrison, Dorothy Nafus. *Chief Sarah: Sarah Winnemucca's Fight for Indian Rights.* Portland: Oregon Historical Society Press, 1990.

Pelz, Ruth. *Women of the Wild West.* Seattle: Open Hand, 1995.

## Periodicals

"The Stone and Kelsey Massacre on the Shores of Clear Lake in 1849: The Indian Viewpoint," *California Historical Society Quarterly* 11, no. 3 (September 1932).

Lucy Young, "Out of the Past: A True Indian Story," *California Historical Society Quarterly* 20, no. 4 (December 1941).

*New York Herald*, December 1848–February 1850.

# Index

# Photography Credits